BEADED HOME

BEADED HOME

25 stunning accessories for every room

Catherine Woram

hamlyn

First published in Great Britain in 2007 by Hamlyn,
a division of Octopus Publishing Group Ltd,
2–4 Heron Quays, London E14 4JP

Distributed in the United States and Canada by
Sterling Publishing Co., Inc., 387 Park Avenue
South, New York, NY 10016-8810

ISBN-13: 978-0-600-61600-9
ISBN-10: 0-600-61600-2

A CIP catalogue record for this book
is available from the British Library.

Printed and bound in China

10 9 8 7 6 5 4 3 2 1

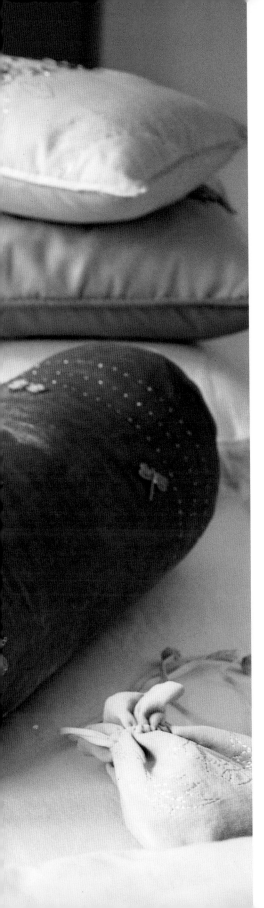

Contents

Introduction   6

Sumptuous soft furnishings   20

Wirework wonders   52

Pretty accents   96

Index   142

Acknowledgements   144

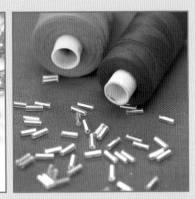

INTRODUCTION

Introduction

Beads are not just for jewellery and accessories: they have long been used to create decorative items for the home, from ornate tassels to cushions and chandeliers. The projects in this book cover many techniques and applications, producing stunning pieces to add richness and sparkle to your home. There is nothing more satisfying than creating something yourself, and each project can easily be adapted to suit the interior of your home by altering colours or substituting different fabrics.

The versatility of beads is enormous – they can be threaded, wired and pinned; they can also be used to embellish fabrics and added to embroidery. You may already have a collection of beads that you can utilize, but if not, start collecting as soon as you can. Secondhand shops, flea markets and sales are a good source of small beads – buy bracelets and necklaces and unthread them. Soak the beads in warm water with a little detergent to clean them. Look in your jewellery box for items that you never wear – these can be recycled. And of course there are many craft shops, haberdashery departments, specialist bead shops and online suppliers where you will find a wide selection of beads.

Beads come in many shapes and sizes. Bugle beads (miniature tubes) and rocaille beads (tiny glass beads) are both types of seed beads that are frequently used for embroidery and textiles as they are light, easy to use both for sewing and wiring, and available in a stunning array of colours. Rocaille beads are usually made of coloured glass, so they produce a shimmering effect, but look out for them in matt finishes, which can be equally effective.

Bugle beads, rocaille beads, pearl beads and sequins have all been used to great effect in the chapter on 'Sumptuous soft furnishings'. Here you will discover how to create a luxurious throw, a tasselled velvet bolster cushion,

embellished contemporary cushions, a fringed taffeta curtain and a beaded summer table runner.

The craft of threading beads on to wire and twisting them into delicate forms dates back to the fifteenth century. The 'Wirework wonders' chapter is devoted to this winning combination of wire and beads, which can be used to great decorative effect. From delicate curtain tiebacks to chunky napkin rings, from beaded votives to wrapped salad servers, and from decorated coffee spoons to embellished vases, these are great projects to make as gifts for friends and family as well as for your own home.

The 'Pretty accents' chapter features a selection of beaded accessories that are bound to attract compliments: a decorated picture frame, an embellished photograph album, beaded coasters and decorations for festive occasions. Turn your bedroom into a beaded boudoir with chic jewelled pieces such as the vintage beaded mirror, French-style lampshade, baroque treasure box and beaded nightlight holders.

Before embarking on the projects, it is recommended that you put together a selection of basic equipment such as scissors, needles and pliers, and materials such as wire and glue (see pages 10–11). Most craft shops have sections devoted to beading and jewellery-making, and also stock handy boxes with separate compartments, which are perfect for managing a bead collection. It can be very frustrating when beads escape from their packaging, so it is advisable to decant beads carefully before beginning a project. Another good tip is to always buy a few more beads than the number specified, in case one gets lost or rolls under the sofa.

You are sure to find beading an absorbing, rewarding and mildly addictive pastime, but most important of all, it is great fun!

Beading basics

You only need a small selection of tools for beading: some of the projects require a needle and scissors; for others pliers are necessary. In some cases a sewing machine and tape measure will also be useful. Thread, wire and glue are the basic construction materials that underpin the decorative materials – beads and sequins.

Tools

Small scissors (1) A good pair of small, sharp scissors is essential for trimming threads close to beading and embroidery work. They can also be used to snip very fine wire and nylon thread.

Dressmaking scissors These large scissors are used for cutting fabrics such as silk, cotton and velvet in projects that involve making up items such as cushions and throws to decorate with beading and embroidery.

Needle-nosed pliers (2) Tapered pliers such as these are useful for coaxing needles through beads, as well as for bending wires. They are used in many projects in the book and it is worthwhile investing in a good-quality pair.

Wire cutters These tools use pressure to cut wires cleanly. Most are hand-held and similar to pliers. In fact, many pliers also include some form of wire-cutting feature.

Lighting Always work in a bright, well-lit area so that you can easily see tiny beads and the eye of the needle.

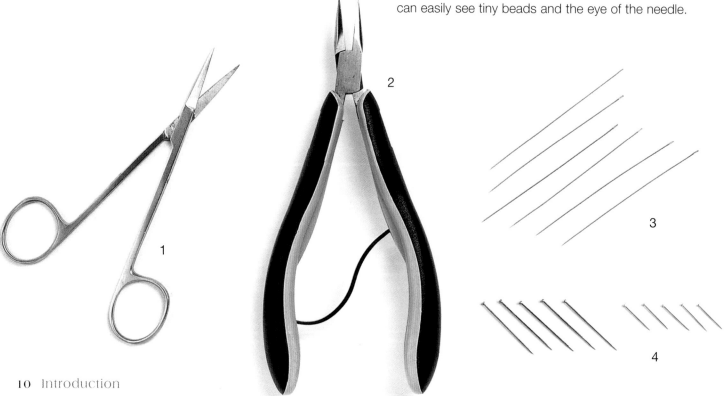

1

2

3

4

Beading needles (3) A beading needle is longer and more flexible than an ordinary dressmaking needle (the head of which is often too large to fit through tiny beads such as rocailles). These needles come in a range of sizes suitable for embroidering with beads and for making beaded fringes.

Pins (4) Pins are used for making items where beads are pinned in place, such as decorated polystyrene balls. Ordinary dressmaking pins, which are about 25–30 mm (1–1³⁄₁₆ in) long, are suitable for most beads. Lill pins are about 13 mm (½ in) long. These very short pins are ideal for pinning rocaille beads in position.

Materials

Headwires and eye pins (5) These long pins are blunt at one end and have a flat head at the other end. They are used to make bead hangers (see the Beaded Chandelier, pages 58–63) – beads are threaded on and the head on the pin stops them falling off; the other end has a flat head or is formed into a hook or a loop. Headwires and eye pins are available in gold and silver.

Nylon thread (6) Clear nylon thread is strong and perfect for projects that require something sturdier than ordinary sewing thread. It is fine enough to fit through many beads and because it is slightly stiffer than sewing thread, it is easy to slip beads on it without using a needle.

Sewing thread Standard sewing thread is used for the projects that involve stitching beads to fabric. It is advisable to use double thread to secure the beads.

Wire (7) Wire is available in different thicknesses (known as gauges) and comes in silver, gold and copper; also metallic colours including blue and red. The finer the wire, the easier it is to twist and shape into decorative objects. Thick wire requires the use of pliers and a certain amount of hard work.

Glue (8) Choose glue according to the type of materials that have to be stuck together, for example, glass to metal, and read the manufacturer's directions to discover which materials a glue is intended to bond. Instant bond glue, or superglue, is very strong and both quick and easy to use. Epoxy glue is mixed from two parts to produce a glue used to stick non-porous materials such as metal and glass together. It should be used in a well-ventilated area. PVA glue is a white liquid, most commonly used for paper and card. It is good for sticking polystyrene, which melts if other glues are used. Fabric glue dries to a clear and flexible finish and, as its name suggests, is designed for bonding fabrics.

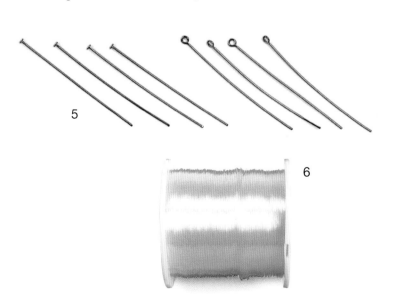

5

6

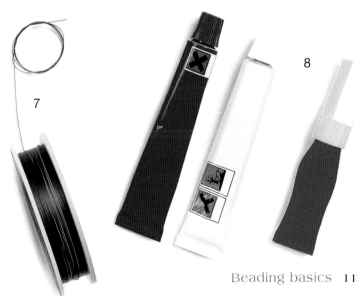

7

8

Beads

Beads are most commonly made of glass, plastic or wood; however, other more unusual materials, such as bone, seeds and stone, also make interesting beads. For some of the projects in this book, the weight of a particular type of bead has to be taken into consideration if a large number of beads is to be used, particularly if they are to be attached to a piece of fabric. Plastic beads are much lighter than glass and may be more suitable. When purchasing beads, be aware that not all colours are permanent. If you are concerned about this, ask the supplier for information.

Assortment of artists' glass beads

Hand-painted

Hand-decorated

Hand-painted and hand-decorated glass beads These are available in a fantastic array of designs in plain and metallic colours. Because they are painted and decorated by hand they are all slightly different, and produce a great individualistic effect. These beads can be expensive, but are the perfect choice for small items such as napkin rings, which do not require many beads.

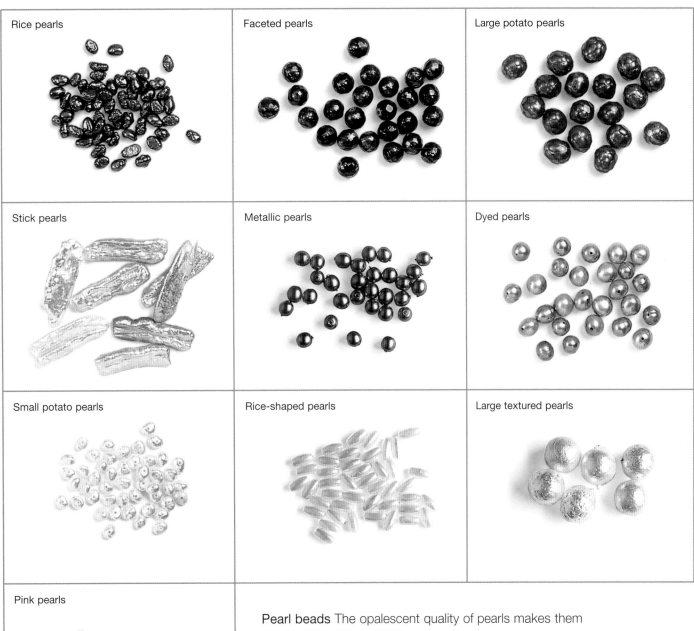

Rice pearls

Faceted pearls

Large potato pearls

Stick pearls

Metallic pearls

Dyed pearls

Small potato pearls

Rice-shaped pearls

Large textured pearls

Pink pearls

Pearl beads The opalescent quality of pearls makes them visually appealing; as well as the classic creamy ivory colour, they come in shades of grey, pink, blue and mauve. Due to the cost of the real thing, pearl beads tend to be plastic, but the finish is deceptively good. They are made in many sizes, and finishes range from a smooth to a textured surface. Real seed pearls are more expensive than their plastic counterparts, but you may decide to use them if a project requires only a small quantity.

Rocaille beads Rocailles are tiny glass beads, rather like seeds, which are both cheap and versatile. They are available in a variety of colours and finishes, such as clear glass, colour-lined translucent versions, matt and silver.

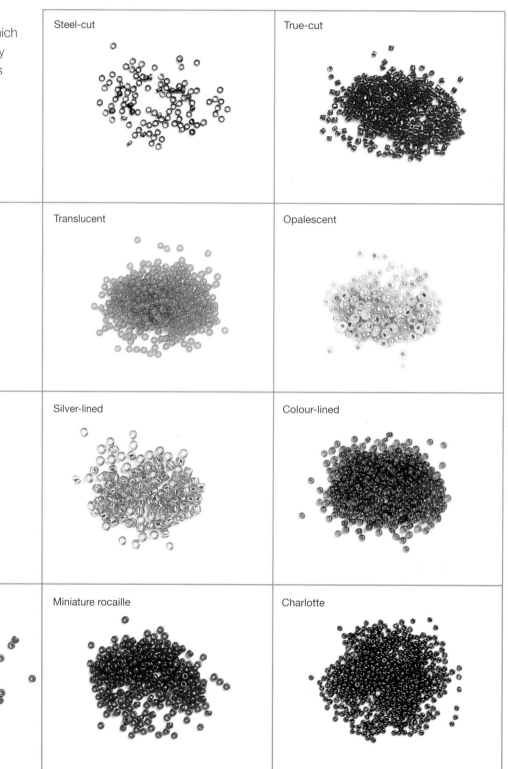

Steel-cut

True-cut

Iridescent tri-cut

Translucent

Opalescent

Greasy opaque

Silver-lined

Colour-lined

Matt iridescent opaque

Miniature rocaille

Charlotte

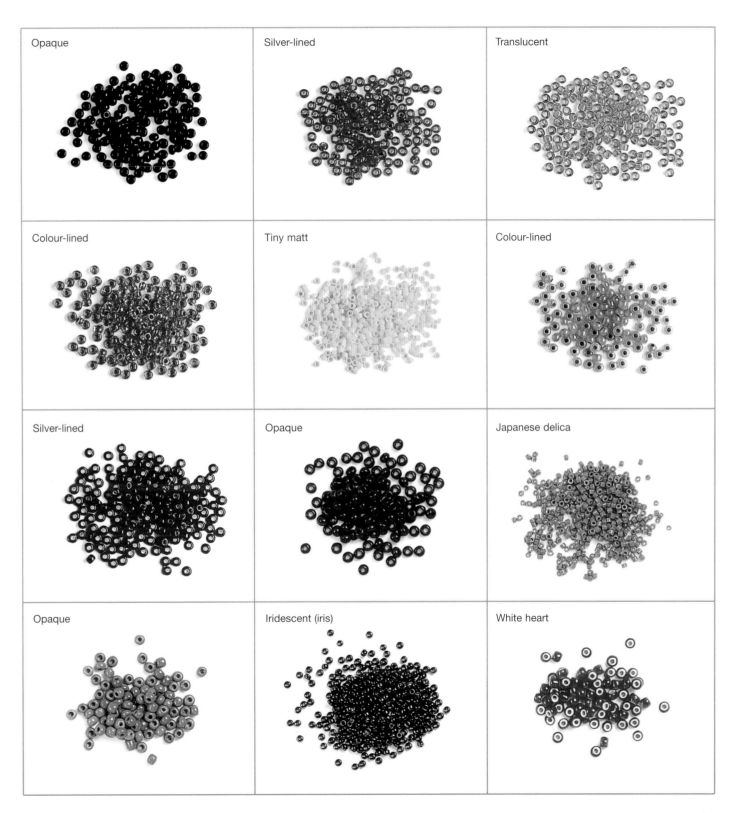

Opaque

Silver-lined

Translucent

Colour-lined

Tiny matt

Colour-lined

Silver-lined

Opaque

Japanese delica

Opaque

Iridescent (iris)

White heart

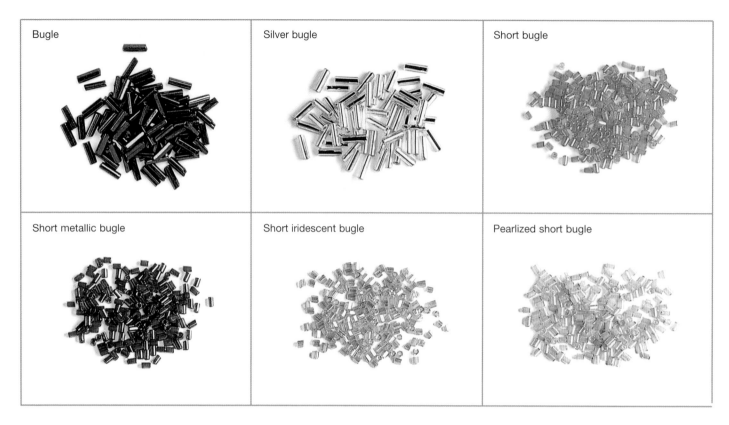

| Bugle | Silver bugle | Short bugle |
| Short metallic bugle | Short iridescent bugle | Pearlized short bugle |

Bugle beads Bugle beads are also made from glass; they are a tubular shape and can be applied to fabrics or threaded on fine wire. The standard length of a bugle bead is approximately 5 mm (3⁄16 in), but it is possible to find longer and shorter versions. The beads are made in a range of colours and can be translucent, opaque or feature a silver lining.

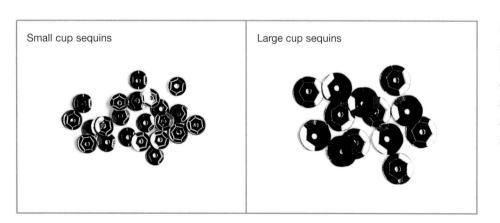

| Small cup sequins | Large cup sequins |

Sequins Although not strictly beads, sequins are frequently paired with beads to create decorative embroidered items. Sequins are available in a vast array of colours, as flat, circular shapes or cup shapes with faceted edges.

Oval

Briolette and pear-shaped

Coin

Rondelle

Nail head

Faceted beads Faceted beads are available in both glass and plastic. They come in a wide selection of sizes, shapes and colours. It is often best to use plastic versions for certain projects, as they are much lighter in weight and more robust than their glass counterparts. They are good for creating a period effect, as they resemble crystal beads. Faceted beads are generally circular, oval or teardrop in shape and look particularly good teamed with pearls.

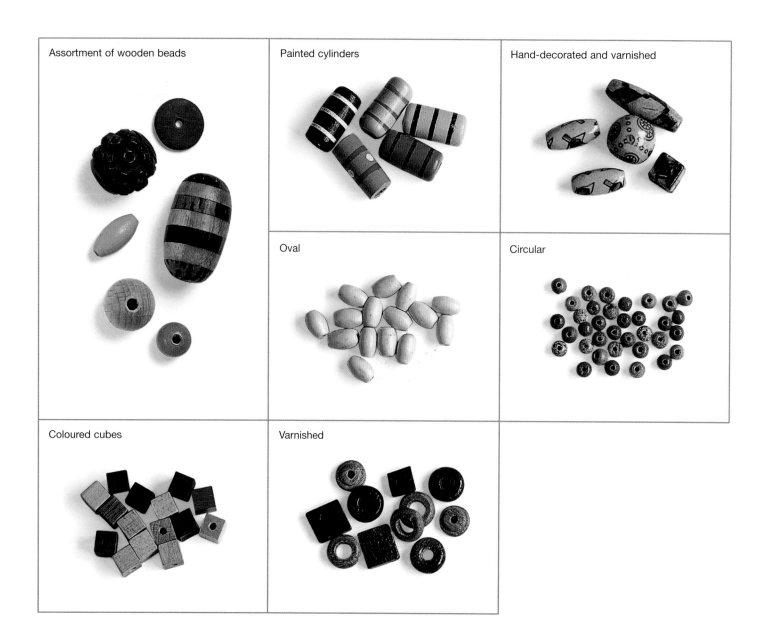

Assortment of wooden beads	Painted cylinders	Hand-decorated and varnished
Oval	Circular
Coloured cubes	Varnished

Wooden beads Wooden beads rely on the shades and grain of wood for their appeal and can be varnished, stained or left in their natural state; sometimes they are also carved. Alternatively the beads may be dyed in bright colours or painted with eye-catching designs. Shapes include cubes, cylinders, spheres, ovals and triangles. Brightly coloured wooden beads are ideal for projects that will appeal to children.

Silver-lined cylinders

Silver-lined cubes

Colour-lined

Cut-glass melon

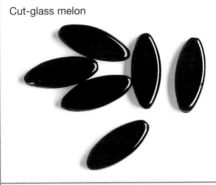

Octagonal faceted

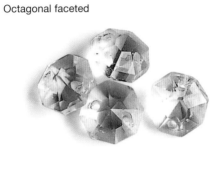

Flowers

Round opaque

Glass beads Glass beads come in many shapes, sizes and colours, from simple spheres and cubes to flower-shapes and translucent coloured beads with silver lining. They are heavier, more delicate and more expensive than plastic beads and therefore unsuitable for certain projects.

SUMPTUOUS SOFT FURNISHINGS

Tropical cushion cover

Patterned and floral fabrics can be made to look richer and more decorative by applying sequins and beads to complement the design. For example, you can trim the edges of petals, or bead around leaf shapes and in the centre of flowers. Buy washable beads and sequins.

You will need

Materials
Floral cushion cover, or fabric to make a
   cushion cover
Assorted cup sequins in bright colours
Assorted rocaille beads and short bugle
   beads in bright colours
Matching sewing threads

Tools
Scissors
Dressmaking pins
Fine needle
Sewing machine

How to make

1 If necessary, make a cushion cover. Cut two pieces of fabric the size of the cushion pad plus 16 mm (⅝ in) turnings on each edge. With the right sides together, pin the edges of the fabric and tack in place. Using a sewing machine, stitch a 16 mm (⅝ in) seam around all the edges, leaving an opening on one edge to turn the cushion cover to the right side.

2 Trim and notch the corners of the fabric and turn the cushion cover to the right side through the opening. Press the cover, turning in the edges of the opening.

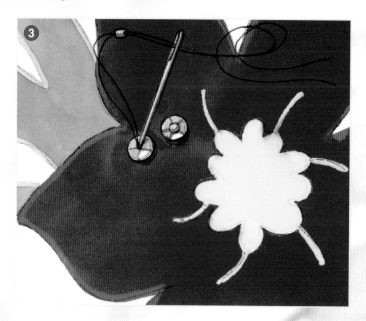

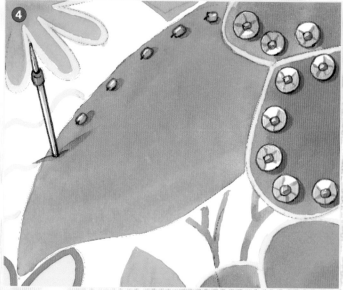

3 To decorate a flower, thread the needle with double thread and knot the end. Working from the back to the front, push the needle through the fabric. Thread on one sequin followed by one rocaille bead, then push the needle back through the centre of the sequin to secure the rocaille. Repeat around the flower.

4 To decorate a leaf with a row of rocaille beads, thread a needle with double thread and knot the end. Working from the back to the front, push the needle through the fabric. Thread on one bead, then push the needle back through the fabric just by the bead. Continue to stitch the beads around the leaf shape in this way at intervals of about 5 mm (3/16 in).

5 To decorate a flower like the daffodil shown in this project, follow the method in step 3 for the petals. To apply bugle beads to the outside of the trumpet, follow the method for step 4, but place the beads in rows that align with the shape of trumpet. For the inside of the trumpet, apply the beads randomly.

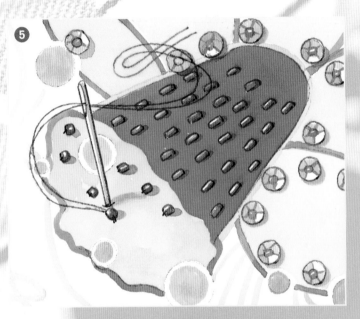

6 Let the patterns on the fabric inspire the way you bead it – the more beading there is, the richer and more multilayered the appearance.

7 If you have made your own cushion cover, put it on the cushion pad. Slipstitch the edges of the opening to close it. (You will need to undo this stitching to remove the cushion cover for washing.)

Glamorous bolster

*This opulent silk velvet bolster cushion is decorated with rows of glass
beads, ribbon motifs and beaded tassels. It looks great on a bed or sofa.
Add more rows of beads to decorate the velvet if desired; another idea is
simply to add the decorative tassels to an existing cushion or bolster.*

You will need

Materials

Bolster cushion:

Silk velvet: 60 x 64 cm (23⅝ x 25³⁄₁₆ in)

Cylindrical bolster cushion pad: 50 cm (19¹¹⁄₁₆ in) long,
 20 cm (8 in) in diameter

Sewing thread to match fabric

Silver glass rocaille beads: 350

Decorative ribbon motifs (dragonflies illustrated here): 12

Tassel (make 2):

Wooden bead for tassel head: 12 mm (½ in) in diameter

Strong sewing thread

Clear fabric glue

Silver glass rocaille beads: 1 per strand of fringe (about
 8 strands in tassel); 250 for covering tassel head

Short silver bugle beads: 8 per strand of fringe

Selection of round and angled faceted plastic crystal-
 effect beads, small and large: 8 per strand of fringe
 in pale pink and clear (about 8 strands in tassel)

Tools

Fine needle

Scissors

Sewing machine

How to make

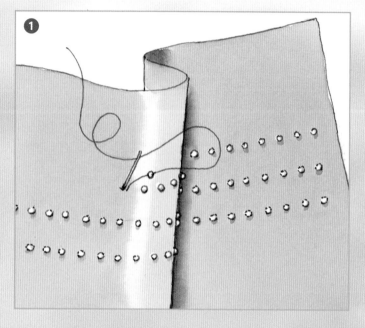

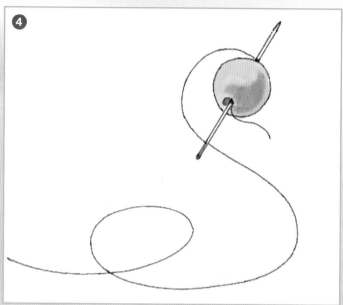

1 Decorate the cushion cover fabric. Stitch three rows of silver glass rocaille beads to the velvet, each row 2 cm (¾ in) apart. The beads should be about 5 mm (³⁄16 in) apart. The first row of beads should be 15 cm (6 in) from the bottom edge of the fabric; work the other two rows towards the centre of the fabric. Repeat at the opposite end of the fabric.

2 Sew the ribbon motifs to the middle part of the fabric, in two rows between the two sections of beading.

3 With right sides together, fold the velvet in half lengthways to make the cushion cover. Machine-stitch a 16 mm (⅝ in) seam along the long edge for approximately 20 cm (8 in) from each end. The central opening is for inserting the bolster cushion pad. Leave the ends open. Turn right side out.

4 Make a beaded tassel, starting with the tassel head. Thread the needle with strong thread and pass it through the wooden bead, over the curve of the bead and back through the hole, then knot the thread. Push the knot into the hole and add a small dab of glue to fix it in place.

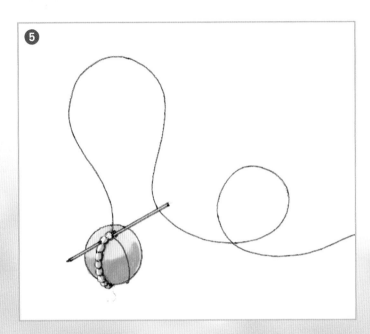

5 Thread sufficient rocaille beads (about ten) on the needle to cover the curved side of the wooden bead. Pass the needle through the hole in the wooden bead, then push the needle through the last two threaded rocaille beads to hold the row in place.

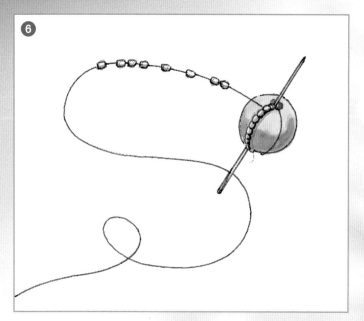

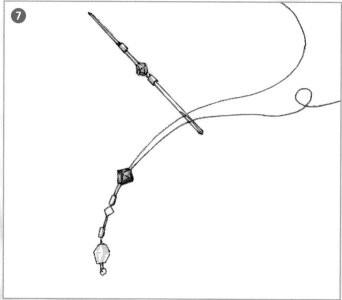

6   For the next row of beads, use two fewer beads than before and repeat the process. Continue around the wooden bead, using ten rocailles followed by eight rocailles in alternate rows. The slight difference in the number of beads per row means that they sit flat on the wooden bead. Cover the whole of the wooden bead. When the last row is complete, thread the needle through the wooden bead and then loop it through the final row to finish off. You may like to add a tiny dab of glue to the end of the thread and push it into the wooden bead to ensure that it does not loosen.

7   Make the tassel end. To make one strand of the fringe, cut a piece of strong thread and slip a rocaille bead on it (this forms the base of the strand). Draw both ends of the thread through a needle. Thread on the bugle beads and crystal-effect beads alternately. Leave the ends of the thread uncut when you have finished. Make approximately eight strands of fringe per tassel.

8 Take the ends of the thread from each strand of fringe and push them through the wooden bead. Tie the ends together to form a tight reef knot, then tie the ends in a reef knot five more times to form a knotted chain. Make another beaded tassel.

9 Fold the ends of the cushion cover to the inside of the fabric, turning in approximately 1.5 cm (9/16 in). Using strong thread, work a running stitch around this edge and pull it to gather the fabric. Before finishing the gathering process, insert the knotted chain of the tassel inside the cushion and stitch it to the fabric. Pull the gathering tightly and stitch it closed. Repeat for the other end.

10 Make a closure for the cushion cover. Turn in 16 mm (5/8 in) along each side of the opening. Insert the bolster cushion. Slipstitch the edges of the opening together.

Modern linen cushion

Decorated with circular shapes drawn in rocaille beads, this cushion makes a modern statement and is simple to create. It would look great in striking black and white, or in neutral shades, substituting small wooden beads for the glass rocaille beads.

You will need

Materials
Linen: 1 piece 42 x 42 cm (16½ x 16½ in),
   1 piece 42 x 25 cm (16½ x 9⅞ in),
   1 piece 42 x 27 cm (16½ x 10⅝ in)
Matching and contrasting sewing thread
Rocaille beads in three different colours:
   approximately 200
Cushion pad 40 x 40 cm (15¾ x 15¾ in)
1 button (optional)

Tools
Assorted plates or circular shapes to use
   as templates
Soft pencil (preferably white)
Fine needle
Scissors
Sewing machine

How to make

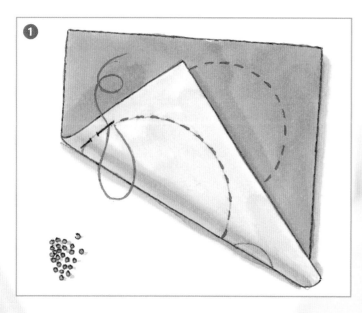

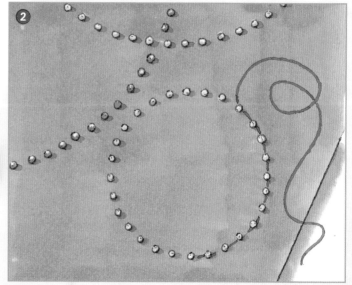

1 Bead the front of the cushion. Turn the large square of fabric to the wrong side and make guidelines for beading by drawing around the circular shapes with the pencil. Stitch around these shapes with large tacking stitches in contrasting sewing thread so that the shapes are visible on the right side of the fabric.

2 Thread the needle with double thread in a matching colour and knot the end. Work around a circle, sewing on rocaille beads in a single colour for each circle. Leave a space of 6 mm (1/4 in) between each bead. Pull out the tacking stitches carefully to avoid loosening the stitched beads.

3 Complete the cushion cover by making the back. The back has a central opening so that the cushion pad can slip inside. Place the two smaller rectangles of fabric with right sides together. On the long edge that will become the central opening, machine-stitch from each end towards the centre for 6 cm (2⅜ in), leaving the centre portion open. The seam should be 5 cm (2 in) from the top edge.

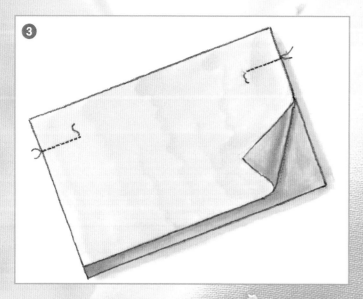

4 Turn the back piece right side out. Fold back the opening edge of the smaller rectangle, so that you end up with an opening where the smaller rectangle laps over the larger rectangle, concealing its edge. Press. Finish the raw edges if desired.

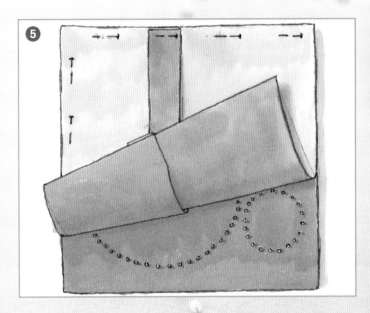

5 Now join the front and back of the cushion cover. Pin the right sides together, then machine-stitch around all four edges with a 2 cm (¾ in) seam. Trim and notch the corners of the fabric and turn right side out. Press. (If required, work a buttonhole on the smaller back rectangle and sew a button on the larger back rectangle to correspond.) Slip the cushion cover on to the cushion pad.

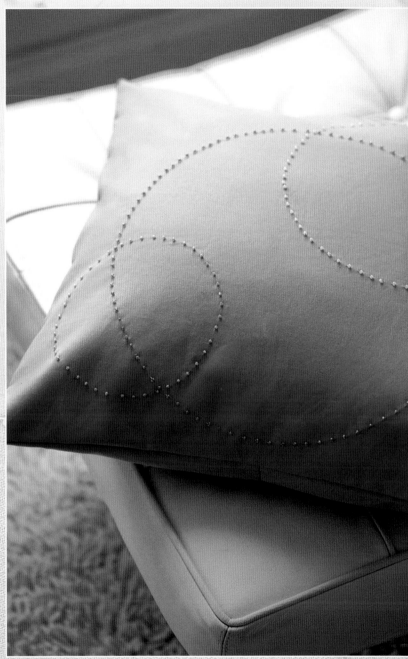

Beaded taffeta curtain

This sumptuous taffeta curtain features a gorgeous beaded fringe, which is made separately on a length of tape and then stitched to the curtain. You could also make matching cushions and table runners, decorated in the same way, for a coordinated look.

You will need

Materials
Taffeta curtain

Matching sewing thread

Cotton tape: 1.5 m (1⅝ yd) (depending on
width of curtain) plus turnings, in colour
to match curtain

Fringe (each strand 1 cm/ ⅜ in apart):
Short bugle beads: 7 per strand

Glass rocaille beads: 7 per strand

Faceted plastic crystal-effect beads (small):
4 per strand

Faceted plastic crystal-effect teardrop
beads: 1 per strand

Tools
Fine needle

Scissors

Sewing machine

How to make

1 To make the first strand of the beaded fringe, thread a needle with a single length of sewing thread and stitch to secure it to one end of the cotton tape. (Don't work on the area for turning).

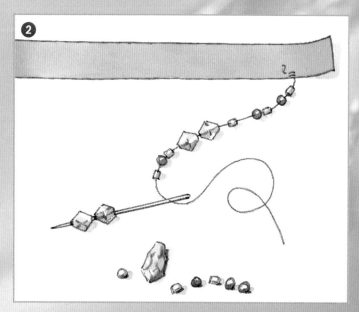

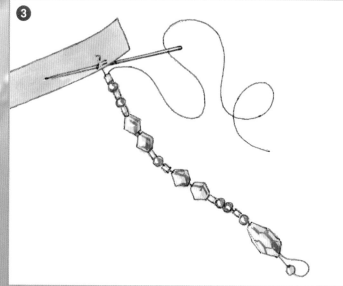

2 Begin threading the beads, starting at what will be the top of the fringe. Thread in the following order: bugle, rocaille, bugle, rocaille, bugle, small crystal, small crystal, bugle, rocaille, bugle, small crystal, small crystal, bugle, rocaille, rocaille, bugle, rocaille, teardrop, rocaille.

3 After the final rocaille bead, thread the needle back through the teardrop and then through all the beads until you reach the top. Bring the needle out through the cotton tape and pull the thread to ensure that it is taut but not too tight. Make several stitches to secure in place.

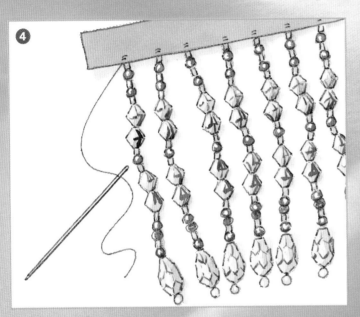

4 Repeat for each strand of the fringe, leaving a space of 1 cm (⅜ in) between each strand. Continue until you have made sufficient strands to fit the length of tape.

Tip

Plastic crystal-effect beads are cheaper and lighter than glass, making them perfect for this project, because it prevents the curtain from becoming too heavy.

You can vary the lengths of each strand of the fringe slightly: by making some strands shorter, you will get a wavy effect.

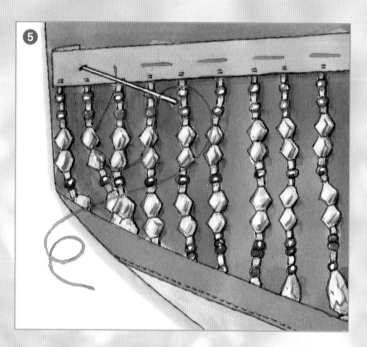

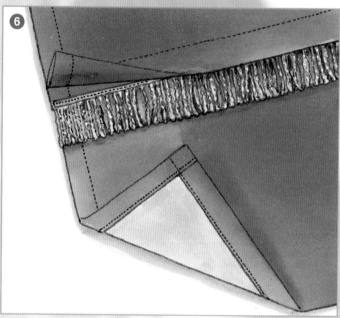

5 Tack the beaded fringe to the right side of the curtain, approximately 48 cm (18⅞ in) from the hem of the curtain. Machine-stitch in place.

6 Make a pleat to disguise the cotton tape. Measure 8 cm (3⅛ in) up the curtain from the top of the cotton tape, and fold the fabric over with wrong sides together. Press a crease across the width of the curtain. Machine-stitch through both layers of the curtain 3 cm (1³⁄16 in) above the cotton tape. Fold the pleat down to cover the tape.

Note

The making-up process for this project involves putting a tuck in the curtain, which takes up about 11 cm (4⁵⁄16 in) of fabric. The curtain, therefore, will end up with a drop that is 11 cm (4⁵⁄16 in) shorter than the depth specified by the manufacturer. Please take this into account.

Summer table runner

This fun table runner, in sizzling summer colours, makes a dramatic statement. It is made of hot pink linen, trimmed with orange beaded fringing. The weight of the fringing also has a practical purpose, preventing the runner from blowing in the wind when it is used outdoors.

You will need

Materials

Cotton tape: length as for width of runner
  plus turnings, x 2, 1 cm (⅜ in) wide
Large rocaille beads: 38 per strand of fringe
  (each strand about 1 cm/ ⅜ in apart);
  100 along topstitching; 46 for applying
  decorative glass beads
Matching sewing thread
Linen fabric: length of table plus 30 cm
  (11¾6 in) drop at each end, 60 cm
  (23⅝ in) wide
Decorative glass beads: 46

Tools

Fine needle
Scissors
Sewing machine

How to make

1 Make the fringing using the rocaille beads and cotton tape. Cut two pieces of tape, the width of the runner plus turnings. To make the first strand of the fringe, thread a needle with a single length of thread and stitch to secure it to one end of the cotton tape (don't work on the area for the turning). Thread on 38 beads. Push the needle back through the second to last bead and then up through all the beads, bringing it out of the cotton tape. Pull the thread to ensure that it is taut but not too tight. Make several stitches to secure in place. Repeat for each strand of the fringe, leaving a space of 1 cm (3⁄8 in) between each strand. Continue until you have made sufficient strands to fit the length of tape.

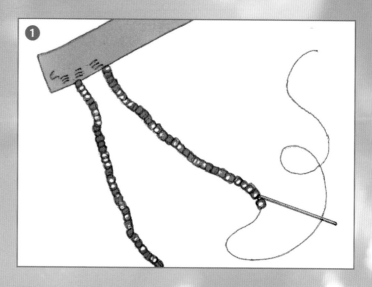

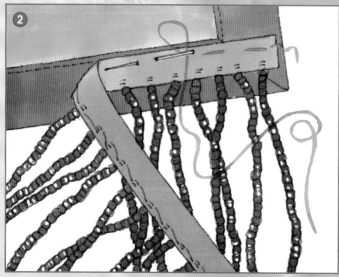

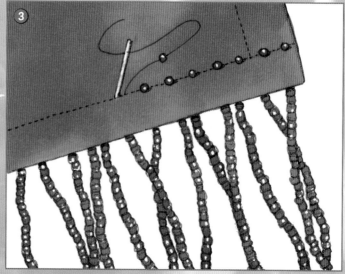

2 Turn in a hem 2 cm (3⁄4 in) deep on all sides of the table runner; press, then open out. Finish the raw edges. Fold the hem under again and topstitch in place using a sewing machine. Tack the fringing to the wrong side of each end of the runner, placing the beaded edge of the tape about 1 cm (3⁄8 in) above the bottom of the runner. Turn in the ends of the tape to neaten. Topstitch with the sewing machine.

3 On the front of the table runner, stitch a row of rocaille beads along the topstitching at each end of the table runner, approximately 3 cm (1 3⁄16 in) from the bottom edge of the fabric. Leave a gap of approximately 1 cm (3⁄8 in) between each bead.

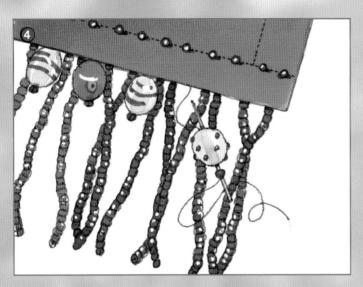

4 Embellish the fringed edges of the runner by stitching on decorative glass beads. To apply the first bead, make a few stitches at the edge of the fabric between the first two strands of the fringe, then thread on a glass bead followed by a rocaille bead. Thread the needle back through the glass bead so that the rocaille holds the thread in place. Finish off at the edge of the fabric by making a few stitches on top of each other. Repeat to apply more decorative glass beads along the edge of the runner.

Elegant throw

This graceful throw, with its delicate pearl and glass flowers and silvery beaded fringe, will add a touch of class to a sofa or armchair. The soft pink and ivory shades make a subtle statement, but the throw would work equally well in richer tones of bronze and gold or turquoise and green.

You will need

Materials
Plain, off-white throw; or linen fabric to make
  throw: 1.5 m (1⅝ yd), 137 cm (54 in) wide
Decorative ribbon: length as for width of
  throw plus turnings; or 1.5 m (1⅝ yd) plus
  turnings for linen fabric, 10 cm (4 in) wide
Cotton thread
Short bugle beads: 220 in soft pink and
  beige, 460 in mauve
Pearl beads: 120 in pale pink and pale
  grey, 4 mm (³⁄16 in) in diameter
Silver glass bugle beads: 12 per strand
  of fringe (each strand about 5 mm/
  ³⁄16 in apart)
Silver rocaille beads: 13 per strand of fringe
  (each strand about 5 mm/ ³⁄16 in apart)
Cotton tape: length as for width of throw
  plus turnings; or 1.5 m (1⅝ yd) plus
  turnings for linen fabric, 1 cm (³⁄8 in)
  wide, off-white

Tools
Fine needle
Scissors
Sewing machine

How to make

1 (If using linen to make the throw, hem the two long edges and one short edge.) Tack the decorative ribbon trim to the throw, with the lower edge approximately 14 cm (5½ in) from the bottom of the fabric (the unfinished edge of the linen). Fold the ends over to the wrong side of the throw, turn in to neaten, and slipstitch to the hem. Topstitch the ribbon in place using a sewing machine.

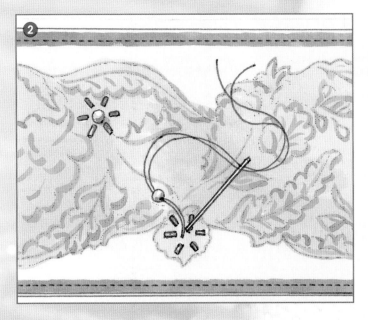

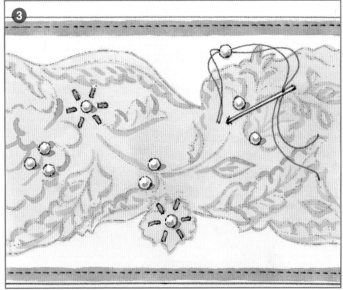

2 Bead the ribbon trim, using double thread for beading. Work flowers using six short mauve bugle beads, pushing the needle through both ribbon and fabric. Sew a pearl bead to the centre of each flower to finish.

3 Sew pearl beads, in groups of two and three, at evenly spaced intervals between the beaded flower shapes. Stitch two rows of short soft pink and beige bugle beads along each edge of the ribbon, about 1 cm (⅜ in) apart, to complete the decoration of the ribbon.

4 Make the fringing from the silver bugle beads and rocaille beads. To make the first strand of the fringe, thread a needle with a single length of thread and stitch to secure it to one end of the cotton tape (don't work on the area for the turning). Begin threading the beads, starting with a rocaille bead at the top of the fringe. Follow this with a bugle bead, then alternate until the strand is about 7.5 cm (3 in) long, finishing with a rocaille bead.

5 Thread the needle back through the second to last bead and then up through all the beads, bringing it out of the cotton tape. Pull the thread to ensure that it is taut but not too tight. Make several stitches to secure in place. Repeat for each strand of the fringe, leaving a space of 5 mm (3⁄16 in) between each strand. Continue until you have made sufficient strands to fit the length of tape.

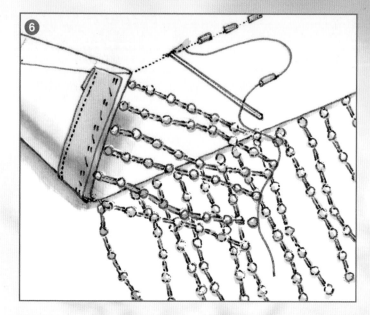

6 On the bottom edge of the throw, fold 4 cm (19⁄16 in) to the wrong side to make a hem. Press, then open out. Tack the fringing to the right side of the bottom of the throw, placing the fringed side of the cotton tape about 5 mm (3⁄16 in) away from the fold, and turning under the ends to neaten. Machine-stitch the unfringed edge of the tape to the hem. Fold the hem to the back of the throw and hand-stitch it in place. On the right side of the throw, sew short soft pink or beige bugle beads along the hemline to cover the stitching.

WIREWORK
WONDERS

Flower tiebacks

Silvery wire and glass rocaille beads are twisted together to form these delicate curtain tiebacks. Although the wire is fine, repeated twisting makes it stronger. You could add coloured beads to echo colours in the curtains, or to match the colour scheme in the room.

You will need

Materials

To make a 1.5 m (1¾ yd) tieback

Fine, silver-coloured wire, 0.4 mm gauge: 15 m (16⅜ yd) per tieback, depending on length required

Glass rocaille beads: 1 x 24 g (1 oz) pot

Larger round glass beads: 116

Tieback hook: 1 per curtain

Tools

Needle-nosed pliers

How to make

1 Cut a length of wire about 3 m (3¼ yd) long and fold it in half. Begin threading beads on one end of the wire (the fold will stop the beads from slipping off). Slide on six rocaille beads, one large bead and then six rocaille beads. Twist into a loop shape to form the first petal of the flower. Twist the wire several times to secure.

2 Make a second petal by threading on six rocailles, one large bead and six rocailles. Twist the wire to secure and repeat to form the third petal of the flower.

3 Twist the two pieces of wire together for about 2 cm (¾ in) to form the stem. Twist as tightly as you can, as this will strengthen the shape.

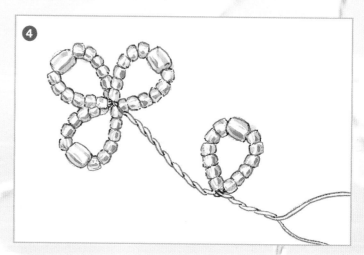

4 Now make a leaf. Thread on six rocailles, one large bead and six rocailles; twist the ends of the wire together to secure. Twist the two pieces of wire together for about 2 cm (¾ in) to form more of the stem. Add another leaf.

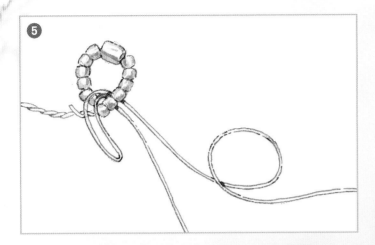

5 Continue adding flowers and leaves, creating three petals for a flower followed by two leaves, until you have made a length of approximately 30 cm (11¹³⁄₁₆ in) for the tieback. (When you need more wire, cut another length, fold it in half and twist it around the base of a leaf or petal to conceal the join.)

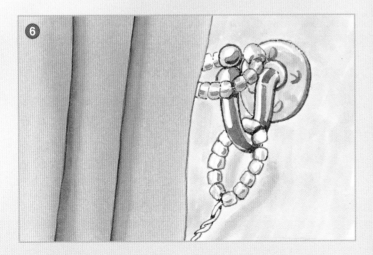

6 Fix the tieback hook to the outer surround of the window, or the wall. Hold the flower tieback around the curtain and pop the final beaded leaf shape at each end of the tieback over the hook to hold the curtain in position.

Beaded chandelier

The restrained colours of this delightful beaded chandelier will harmonize perfectly with a country-style interior. Find a black iron design, spray it ivory and thread on a selection of decorative glass beads using the existing holes in the chandelier.

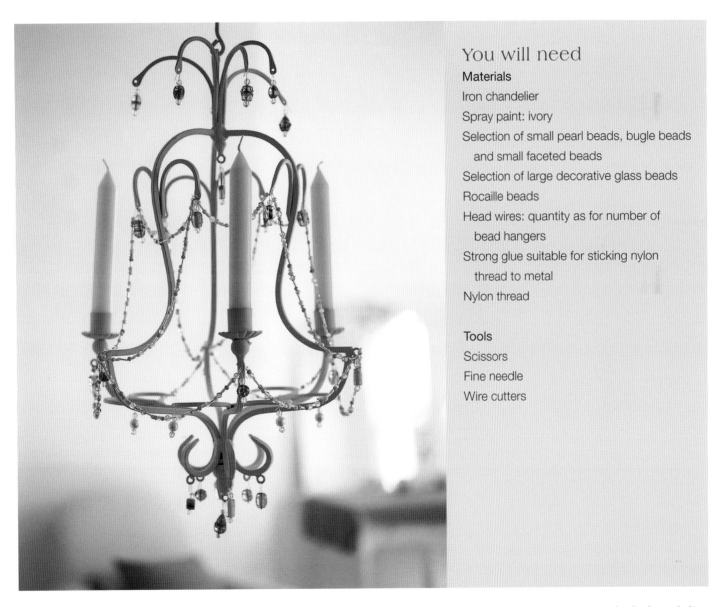

You will need

Materials

Iron chandelier

Spray paint: ivory

Selection of small pearl beads, bugle beads
    and small faceted beads

Selection of large decorative glass beads

Rocaille beads

Head wires: quantity as for number of
    bead hangers

Strong glue suitable for sticking nylon
    thread to metal

Nylon thread

Tools

Scissors

Fine needle

Wire cutters

How to make

1 Spray the chandelier with paint and leave it to dry (do this outdoors).

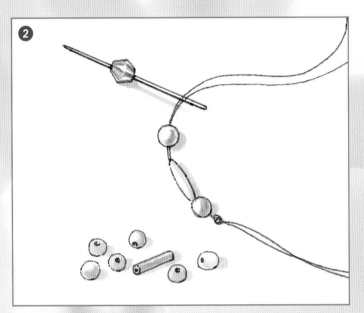

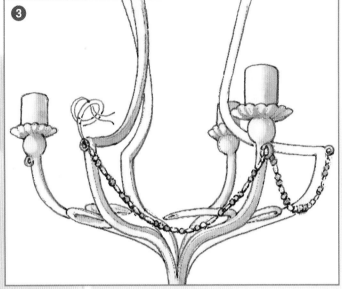

2 Start making strings of beads to loop between parts of the chandelier. To create a loop shape, a string of beads should be approximately 2 cm (¾ in) longer than the straight distance between the two holes on the chandelier. Thread the needle with a double length of nylon thread and tie a knot 4 cm (1⁹⁄₁₆ in) from the bottom of the thread ends. Begin threading on the pearls, bugle beads and faceted beads.

3 When you have completed the string of beads, loop each end of the thread through the hole in the chandelier and tie together several times in a knot. Add a small dab of glue to the knot to secure it. Make both horizontal and vertical beaded loops, depending on the shape of the chandelier. Each time you knot the nylon thread, add a dab of glue to ensure that the knots do not come undone.

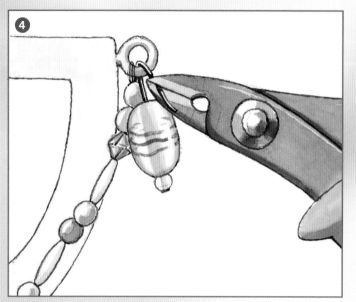

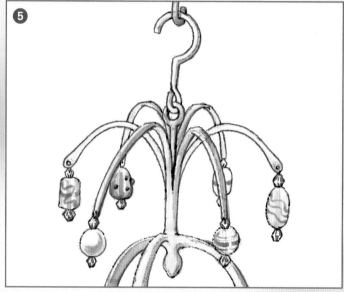

4 Now make little bead hangers to add a final decorative touch to the chandelier. Take a head wire, thread on a rocaille bead and follow it with a large decorative glass bead. Thread the top of the wire through a hole in the chandelier and fold the wire over to form a hook. Trim the end of the head wire so that the hook is about 1 cm (3/8 in) long. Repeat as required.

5 Make another type of bead hanger by threading on a small faceted bead, then a large decorative glass bead, then another small faceted bead. Fix to the chandelier as before. Repeat as required.

Note
You may need to adjust the quantities of beads and other materials used, depending on the design of your chandelier.

Wrapped salad servers

These salad servers are wrapped with fine wire and decorated with coloured glass beads, turning simple utensils into something altogether more interesting. You could even use coloured wire, which is available from many craft shops, with contrasting beads for a really zingy effect.

You will need

Materials
Salad servers with tubular handles
Silver-plated wire, 0.6 mm gauge:
    approximately 10 m (11 yd) to wrap
Glass beads with flat backs: 5 per server
Silver-plated wire, 0.4 mm gauge: 1 m
    (1⅛ yd) to attach beads
Strong glue suitable for gluing metal

Tools
Needle-nosed pliers

How to make

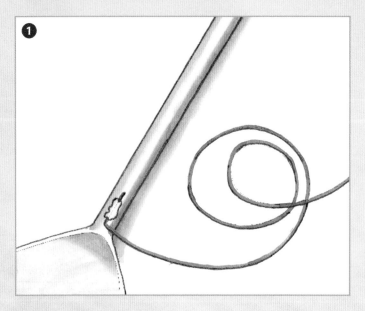

1 First, wire the handles of the salad servers. Glue one end of the 0.6 mm wire to the handle, by the spoon end. Fold the wire upwards.

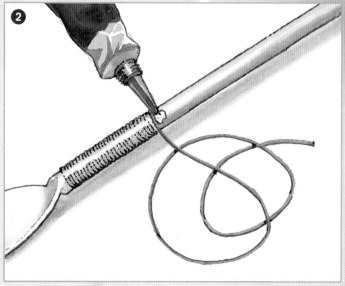

2 Begin winding the wire around the handle. It is easier to turn the utensil rather than the wire, which becomes twisted easily. Apply a dab of glue every 2 cm (¾ in), to hold the wire in place. Wrap from the base of the handle to approximately a quarter of the way up the handle.

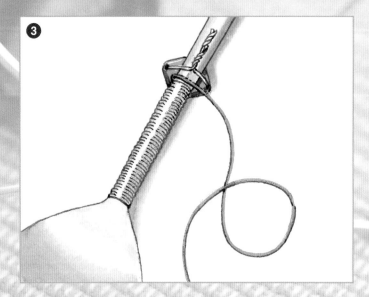

3 To attach the first bead, cut a piece of bead wire 8 cm (3⅛ in) long. Thread it through the bead and place the flat side of the bead against the front of the handle. Twist the ends of the wire together at the back of the handle as tightly as possible. Trim the ends with the pliers, leaving the tails about 2 cm (¾ in) long. Fold the tails upward to lie against the handle.

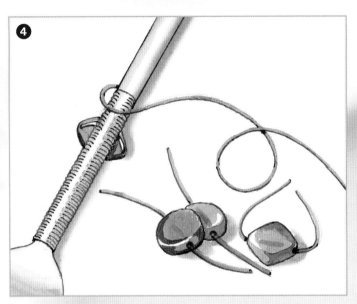

4 Begin winding the wire around the handle again, covering the ends of the bead wire as you go. This will ensure that the bead is held firmly in place.

5 Continue wrapping the wire around the server and add further beads, equal distances apart, as before. Finish wrapping the handle about 2 cm (¾ in) before the end. Cut the end of the wire at the back of the server. Glue the wire to the handle to make sure that it does not unwind. Allow the glue to dry thoroughly before use.

Care instructions

These decorative salad servers should be washed carefully by hand, taking care not to make the decorations too wet. Do not wash them in a dishwasher. Dry immediately after washing.

Chunky spiral napkin rings

A wire spiral threaded with faceted, crystal-effect beads creates a striking napkin ring. The coloured plastic beads used here are inexpensive, lightweight and practical; however, you could use real crystal or glass beads for a truly luxurious effect.

You will need

Materials
Per napkin ring:
Faceted plastic crystal-effect beads: 60
Wire, 1.2 mm gauge: 55 cm (21⅝ in)
Fine wire, 0.4 mm gauge: 50 cm (19¹¹⁄₁₆ in)
Rocaille beads: 2

Tools
Tube-shaped object approx. 4 cm (1⁹⁄₁₆ in)
   in diameter
Needle-nosed pliers

How to make

1 Shape the thick wire into a spiral by wrapping it around the tube-shaped object. Remove the wire carefully from the tube once it has taken a spiral form.

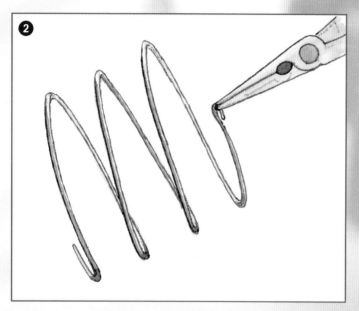

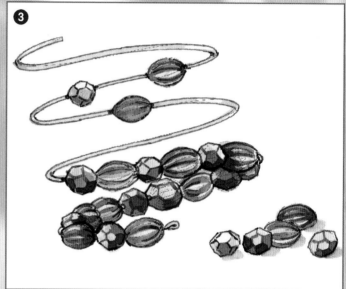

2 Bend one end of the wire into a small loop, using the pliers to pinch it together. This will prevent the threaded beads from falling off the wire.

3 Thread 58 crystal-effect beads on to the spiral, taking care not to pull the wire out of shape. After the final bead, use the pliers to make a small loop at the end of the wire as before.

4 Make a bead trim for each end of the spiral. Thread one crystal-effect bead on a piece of fine wire, followed by one rocaille bead, then thread the wire back through the plastic bead. Pass the ends of the fine wire through the loop at the end of the spiral and twist together to secure. Trim the ends with the pliers to finish. Repeat at the other end of the napkin ring.

Flower coffee spoons

These delicate flowers are made from fine wire and rocaille beads. They look delightful as decorations on the end of tiny coffee spoons, but can also be used to trim decorative boxes, handmade greetings cards and bookmarks. The flowers would be equally pretty made in pearl beads.

You will need

Materials

To make four flower coffee spoons:

Fine wire, 0.4 mm gauge: 4 m (4⅓ yd)

Glass rocaille beads: 200 pink, 200 blue, 200 green, 200 lilac

Pearl beads: 4

Small metal coffee spoons: 4

Strong glue suitable for metal

Tools

Needle-nosed pliers

How to make

1 Cut 1 m (1⅛ yd) of wire per flower. First, make the ring of outer petals. Make a small bend in the wire about 20 cm (8 in) from one end. Thread on 24 rocaille beads and move them along the wire until they reach the bend.

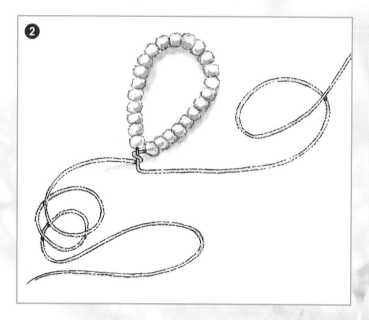

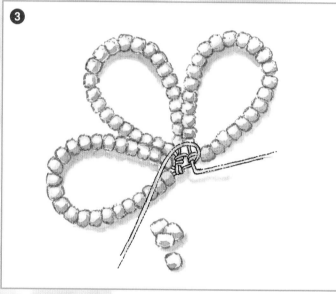

2 Bend the wire to form a loop for the first petal shape. Twist the wire at the bottom of the loop several times to secure the beads.

3 Repeat the process to make four more petals, twisting the wire around the centre of the flower each time to secure the petals.

4 The inner petals are made in the same way as the outer ones, but with fewer beads and smaller loops. Thread on 16 rocaille beads for each petal. Make an inner petal inside each outer petal.

Care instructions
These decorative coffee spoons should be washed carefully by hand, taking care not to make the decorations too wet. Do not wash them in a dishwasher. Dry immediately after washing.

5 To finish the flower, thread a pearl bead on to the 20 cm (8 in) of wire that was kept free in step 1. Pull the wire over the centre of the flower so that the pearl bead sits in this position, covering the mass of twisted wires at the centre. Fold the wire to the back of the flower and twist it together with the other end of the wire. Trim the ends with the pliers.

6 Apply glue to the centre back of the flower to attach it to the end of the spoon. Make three more flowers for the other spoons.

Wall sconce

A ready-made wire wall sconce was sprayed green to create this quirky beaded candleholder. It is garlanded with chains of beads; bead hangers and flower-shaped beads complete the effect. It would work equally well in other colourways such as pale blue or even gold.

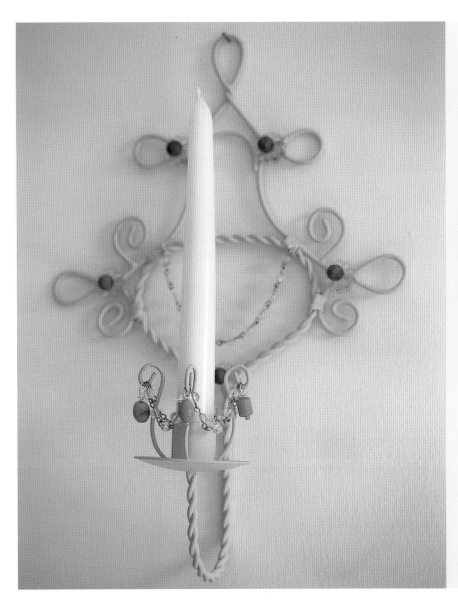

Materials

Wire wall sconce
Spray paint: green
Wire, 0.8 mm gauge: 1.5 m (1⅝ yd)
Fine wire, 0.4 mm gauge: 50 cm (19¹¹⁄₁₆ in)
Small round clear glass beads: 32
Silver head wires: 4 x 5 cm (2 in) long
Oval and/or cylindrical green beads: 4
Green rocaille beads: 4
Flower-shaped clear glass beads: 5
Faceted green beads: 5
Strong glue suitable for fixing glass to metal

Tools

Needle-nosed pliers

How to make

1 Spray the wall sconce with paint and leave it to dry (do this outdoors).

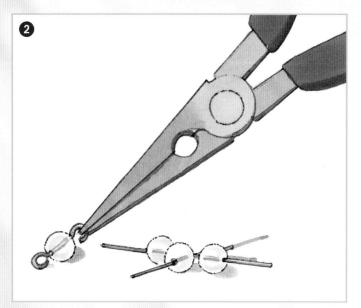

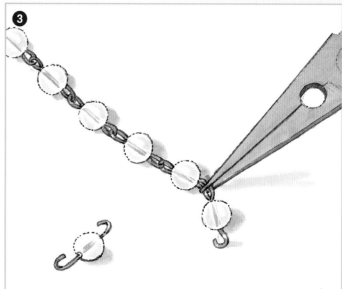

2 Make the beaded chain for the central loop on the sconce. The links of the chain are made of 28 mm (1⅛ in) lengths of 0.8 mm wire. To make the first link, thread a single clear glass bead on a piece of wire and use the pliers to bend the wire into a hook at both ends.

3 Make the next link in the same way, but bend one end of the wire around the hook on the previous link. Repeat until the beaded chain contains 12 beads, finishing each end by bending the wire into a hook.

4 Fix the beaded chain to the sconce with fine wire, threading it through the ends of the chain and wrapping it around the sconce, twisting the ends of the wire together at the back of the sconce to secure them. Trim the ends with the pliers.

5 Now make four short beaded chains to decorate the candleholder, using the same process. Each chain contains five beads. To attach the chains, bend the hook at each end around the wall sconce.

Safety
Never leave a burning candle unattended and always keep candles out of reach of young children.

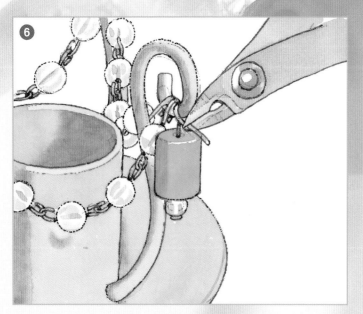

6 Make four bead hangers to add to the candleholder. Take a head wire, thread on a rocaille bead and then an oval or cylindrical green bead. Bend the head wire over the sconce and twist it so that the hanger is securely hooked on. Trim the end of the wire with the pliers.

7 Glue the five glass flowers to the upper part of the sconce, then glue a round green faceted bead to the centre of each flower to finish.

Note
You may need to adjust the quantities of beads and other materials used, depending on the design of your wall sconce.

Spiral beaded votives

These graphic black and white votives, containing a plain white candle, make elegant contemporary table decorations. They are simplicity itself to produce: rocaille beads are threaded on a piece of wire and then wrapped around a glass candle-holder.

You will need

Materials

Per votive:

Glass: about 5 cm (2 in) in diameter and 6 cm (2⅜ in) tall

Fine wire, 0.4 mm gauge: 2.6 m (2⅞ yd)

Glass rocaille beads: 1 x 24 g (1 oz) pot black, 1 x 24 g (1 oz) pot white

Glue suitable for sticking metal to glass

Tools

Needle-nosed pliers

How to make

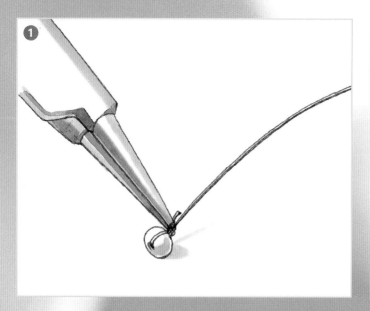

1 Thread one bead on to the end of the wire, bend the end up and twist it to prevent subsequent beads slipping off the wire.

2 Thread on a batch of beads in the same colour. We covered approximately 5 cm (2 in) of the wire in the first colour, but you could use fewer beads if preferred. Thread on a second batch of beads in the other colour. Continue until you have enough beaded wire to wrap around the votive, varying the lengths of each coloured section slightly. At the end of the wire, bend it back and twist it around itself to secure the beads.

Safety
Never leave a burning candle unattended and always keep candles out of reach of young children.

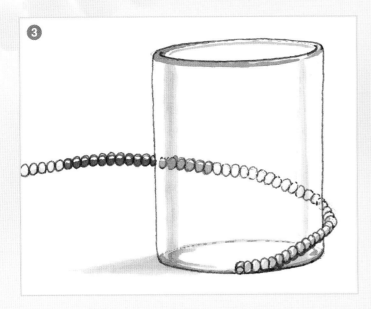

3 Attach the beaded wire to the votive, starting at the bottom of the glass. Apply a dab of glue to keep the end of the wire in place.

4 Wrap the beaded wire around the votive, using a dab of glue every so often to keep it in position. Continue until about 2 cm (¾ in) from the top of the glass. Glue the end to the glass.

Vase decorations

These attractive decorations are similar to earrings in design and can be hung from vases or other ornaments such as metal candlesticks or chandeliers. The combination of pink and yellow beads grabs attention; the alternative design features natural-coloured wooden beads.

You will need

Materials

Per decoration:

Wire, 1.2 mm gauge: 20 cm (8 in)

Small round beads: approx. 5

Larger beads: approx. 5

Tools

Needle-nosed pliers

How to make

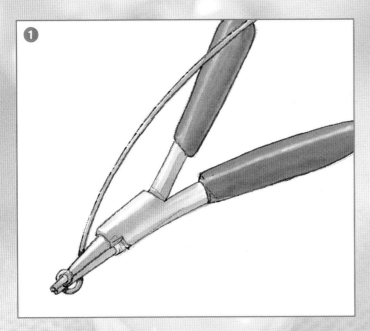

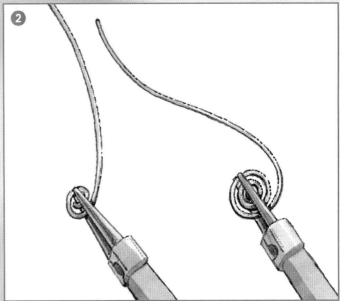

1 Pinch one end of the wire between the pliers and start twisting it to form the centre of the spiral shape that is at the bottom of each decoration.

2 Remove the wire from the pliers, press the pliers over the flat part of the spiral, then continue twisting to form a spiral with a diameter of around 1 cm (⅜ in).

3 Bend the wire at the top of the spiral to form a right angle (this will prevent the beads from slipping down on to the spiral).

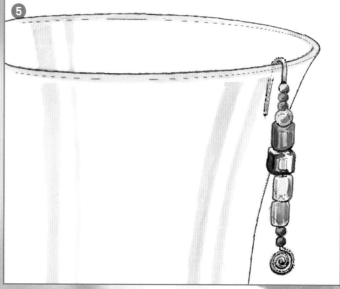

4 Thread two small beads on the wire. Then thread on five large beads, followed by three small beads. We used slightly differing numbers of beads on each decoration to make them look individual.

5 Bend over the top of the wire to form a hook and hang the decoration on the vase. Trim the end of the hook down to around 2 cm (¾ in) to finish.

Wooden bead option

We used little wooden beads, in several sizes, to create slender decorations that work well on a tall, slim vase. You could make them in varying lengths for a different look.

Fancy bead napkin rings

Decorative hand-painted glass beads have been combined to create these stunning napkin rings, which are trimmed with beads attached with fine wire. Look out for antique necklaces that can be unstrung and the beads used to create beautiful new objects such as these.

You will need

Materials

Per napkin ring of 4 cm (1⁹/₁₆ in) diameter:

Glass (or pearl) beads: 12–16, depending on size, for the ring; 5 for trim

Rocaille (or tiny pearl) beads: 5 for trim

Wire, 1.2 mm gauge: 20 cm (8 in)

Fine wire, 0.4 mm gauge: 50 cm (19¹¹/₁₆ in)

Tools

Wire cutters

How to make

1 Make the basic shape of the napkin ring by threading beads on the thick piece of wire until it is full. Thread on beads of alternate shapes and sizes for variety.

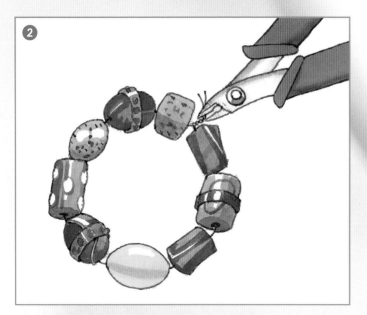

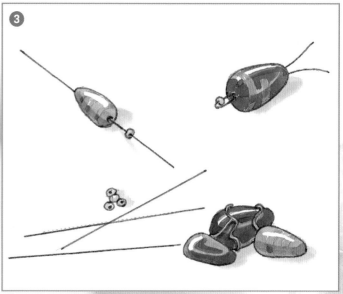

2 Bend the wire into a circle, twist the ends together to secure them and trim with the wire cutters.

3 Make the trim pieces. Cut five lengths of fine wire, 10 cm (4 in) in length. Thread each wire length with a glass bead and a rocaille bead. Thread the wire back through the glass bead.

Pearl bead option

Use the same method to create romantic napkin rings using a selection of different-sized pearl beads in shades of ivory, cinnamon and soft pearly pink.

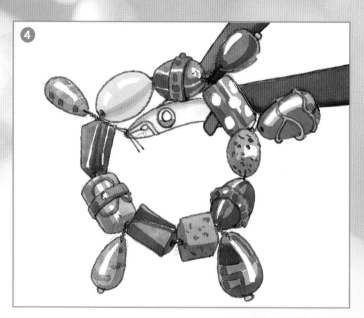

4 Place each trim between two of the beads on the napkin ring, twisting the ends of the wire to secure them to the ring, but ensuring that the wire is slightly loose so that the bead hangs freely from the ring. Cut off the ends of the wire with the wire cutters.

PRETTY
ACCENTS

French-style lampshade

This pretty lampshade is trimmed with loops of pearl beads, which are stitched to the underside of the shade. A sheer ribbon bow and a wired pearl circle complete the chic effect. For a more decorative look, apply two or more loops of beads and add longer beads between each loop.

You will need

Materials

Plain lampshade (we used a shade with a
    diameter of 25 cm/10 in)
Small pearl beads, 4 mm (³⁄₁₆ in) in
    diameter: 10 beads per loop (measure
    circumference of shade – loops spaced
    3 cm/ 1³⁄₁₆ in apart); 13 beads for
    wired circle
Fine wire, 0.4 mm gauge: 10 cm (4 in)
Sheer ribbon: 50 cm (19¹¹⁄₁₆ in)
Matching thread
Clear fabric glue

Tools

Fine needle
Scissors
Wire cutters

How to make

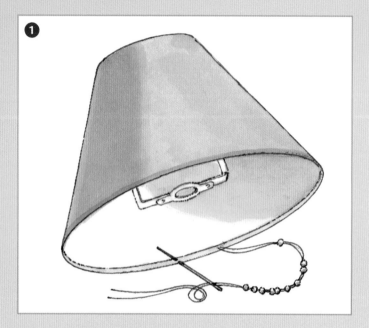

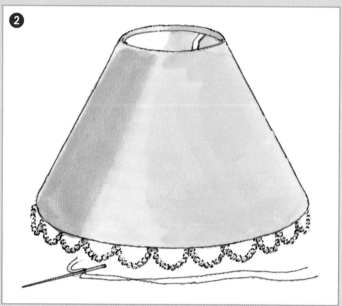

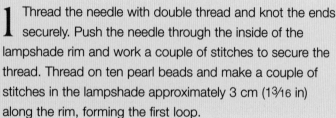

1 Thread the needle with double thread and knot the ends securely. Push the needle through the inside of the lampshade rim and work a couple of stitches to secure the thread. Thread on ten pearl beads and make a couple of stitches in the lampshade approximately 3 cm (1³⁄16 in) along the rim, forming the first loop.

2 Repeat the loops around the entire base of the lampshade. When you reach the end, work several stitches to finish off and tie the ends of the thread in a knot before carefully trimming the ends.

3 Tie the sheer ribbon into a bow and fix to the front of the lampshade with a small dab of glue.

4 Make the pearl circle trim. Thread about 13 pearls on the length of fine wire, bend it into a circle and twist the ends together to secure. Cut the ends of the wire with the wire cutters. Fix the pearl circle to the lampshade with a small dab of glue.

Moroccan-style coasters

These simple coasters are quick and easy to make and will lend a splash of colour to any dining table. Linen in cornflower blue and deep turquoise embellished with silver bugle beads evokes a Moroccan colour scheme, but the coasters would work equally well in neutral or pastel colours.

You will need

Materials

Per coaster:

Linen: 2 squares, 13.5 x 13.5 cm
   (5⅝₁₆ x 5⅝₁₆ in)
Bugle beads: 36
Matching sewing thread

Tools

Soft pencil
Ruler
Fine needle
Dressmaking pins
Sewing machine
Scissors

How to make

1 Take one square of fabric and, using a pencil and ruler, make guidelines for beading by drawing a line on the wrong side of the fabric about 1.5 cm (9/16 in) from the edge of the square.

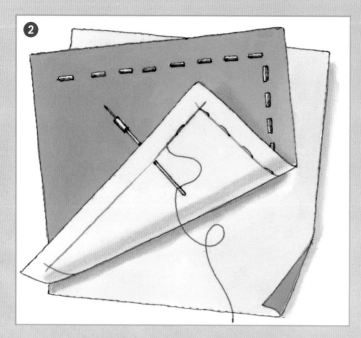

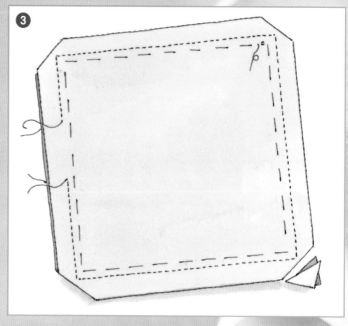

2 Thread a needle with a double length of thread and knot the end. Starting at one corner, stitch a line of bugle beads around the edge of the square, following the guidelines, using a simple running stitch. Leave a gap of about 3 mm (1/8 in) between each bead. To finish, secure the thread on the back of the fabric with three tiny running stitches on the same spot.

3 With the right sides together, pin along the edges of two squares of fabric and tack in place. Using a sewing machine, stitch a 1 cm (3/8 in) seam around all the edges, leaving an opening of about 3 cm (13/16 in) on one edge. Trim and notch the corners of the fabric.

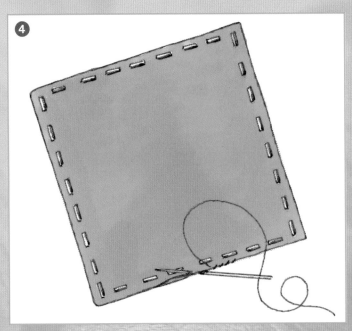

4 Turn the coaster to the right side through the opening. Press the coaster flat, turning in the edges of the opening. Slipstitch the edges of the opening to close it.

Beaded nightlight holders

These pretty nightlights are created by covering plain glass candle-holders with handmade paper and decorating them with a beaded trim on embroidered ribbon. In vibrant lime green and turquoise, they are the perfect accessory for an outdoor dining table in summer.

You will need

Materials

Per nightlight:

Glass: about 7 cm (2¾ in) in diameter and 8 cm (3⅛ in) tall

Handmade paper

Narrow embroidered ribbon: length as for circumference of glass plus 2 cm (¾ in)

Rocaille beads: 20 per loop (loops spaced about 1.5 cm/ 9/16 in apart around circumference; a glass with a diameter of 7 cm/ 2¾ in accommodates 12 loops)

Larger beads: 1 per loop

Fabric glue

Spraymount adhesive

Cotton thread to match beaded trim

Tools

Fine needle

Scissors

How to make

1 Cut a piece of handmade paper to fit the sides of the glass, allowing 2 cm (¾ in) extra on each side. Roll the paper around the glass to make sure it fits.

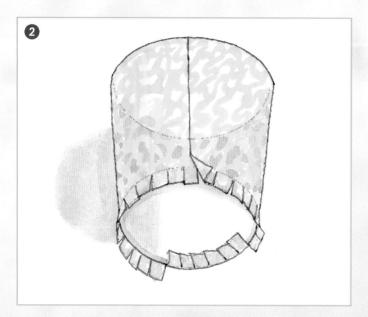

2 Spray a light coating of spraymount adhesive on the wrong side of the paper. Roll the paper around the glass, smoothing it as you go to ensure that there are no creases or bumps. The edges should overlap in the centre of the glass by about 1 cm (⅜ in); trim away the excess. Trim the paper at the top edge of the glass. Allow about 5 mm (³⁄₁₆ in) to fold under the bottom of the glass. Snip this at regular intervals to form tabs to make folding easier.

3 Make the beaded ribbon trim. Thread the needle with cotton and make a couple of stitches at one end of the ribbon, about 1 cm (⅜ in) from the end. Thread ten rocaille beads on the cotton, followed by a large bead, then ten more rocaille beads: this is the first loop. Push the needle through the lower edge of the ribbon, 1.5 cm (⁹⁄₁₆ in) from the first stitches, to form the loop; secure with two more stitches.

Safety
Never leave a burning candle unattended and always keep candles out of reach of young children.

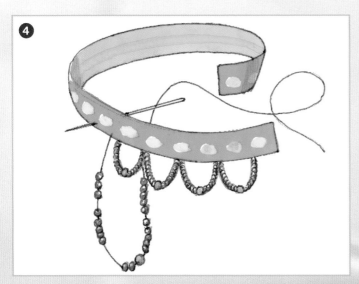

4 Continue to make loops along the ribbon, stopping 1 cm (⅜ in) from the end.

5 Trim 1 cm (⅜ in) from one end of the ribbon. Apply glue to the wrong side of the ribbon and stick it to the top of the glass, folding over the ribbon as you wind it around the circumference to conceal the raw edge of the other end.

Fun picture frame

Bright wooden beads jazz up a plain frame and create an eye-catching feature on a dull wall. Here painted cylindrical beads are used around the inside edge of the frame; square beads are scattered across the frame. Use wooden beads on a plain wood frame for a more natural version.

You will need

Materials

Wooden picture frame

Painted cylindrical wooden beads in assorted colours: number to fit inner edge of frame (36 x 1.5 cm/ 9/16 in beads fit an inner edge of 11.5 x 16.5 cm/ 4½ x 6½ in)

Small square wooden beads: about 25, depending on size of frame

Strong clear glue, suitable for bonding wood

Tools

Soft pencil

Ruler

How to make

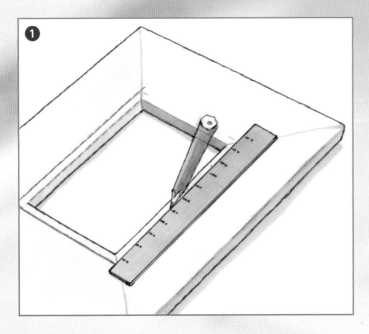

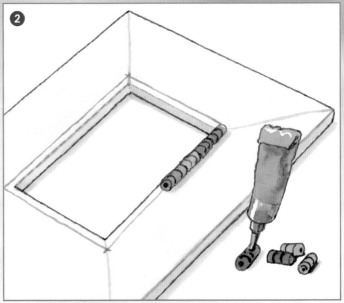

1 Lay the cylindrical beads around the inner edge of the frame to work out how far away from the edge they need to be in order to fit around it without any gaps. Lightly mark the line they need to follow with a pencil and ruler.

2 Apply a dab of glue to the back of a bead and place it carefully on the pencil line. Press firmly in place. Repeat until you have glued all the beads to the inner edge of the frame.

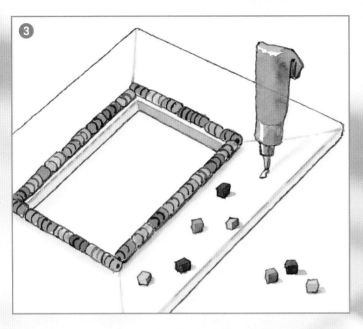

3 Now glue the square beads to the main part of the frame, applying them at random intervals. Allow to dry completely.

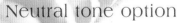

Neutral tone option

We used neutral-toned wooden beads, in several shapes and sizes, on a plain wooden frame for a more natural-looking version (see right).

Shaker-style festive decorations

The simple shapes of hearts and stars create these delightful felt Christmas decorations, which are outlined with tiny rocaille beads in a contrasting colour. Try using the same method to make different shapes such as Christmas trees, Christmas stockings and simple bird motifs.

You will need

Materials

Per decoration:

Felt: 2 x 15 cm (6 in) squares

Matt rocaille beads: 65, in contrasting colour to felt

Polyester stuffing

Matching sewing thread

Cardboard: 2 x 15 cm (6 in) squares

Tools

Pinking shears

Pencil

Fine needle

Scissors

How to make

1 Draw templates for the heart and star on the pieces
of cardboard and cut them out. Place a template on a
square of felt and draw lightly around it with a pencil. Cut
out the shape with pinking shears to give a zigzag edge.
You will need two pieces of each shape per decoration,
to form the front and back.

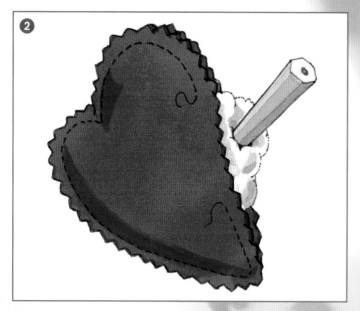

2 Place the front and back together. Using small running
stitches, sew around the decoration 6 mm (¼ in) from
the edge to join the pieces together. Leave a small opening
of 3 cm (1³⁄₁₆ in). Insert the stuffing through the opening,
carefully pushing it in with a pencil, then stitch it to close.

3 Stitch rocaille beads around the edges of the
decoration, to cover the running stitches, leaving
a gap of 5 mm (³⁄₁₆ in) between each bead.

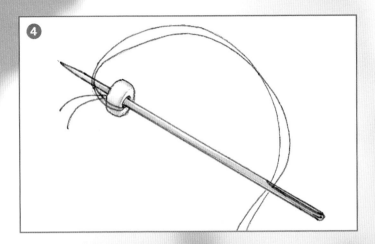

4 To make the hanging loop, thread one rocaille bead on a doubled length of thread and push the needle back through the bead twice to secure it. Add more beads to create a string 14 cm (5½ in) in length.

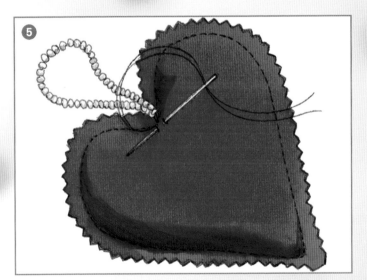

5 Attach the string to the decoration. Push the needle through the back of the decoration, at the top, and work several stitches to secure the string. Bring the other end of the string to lie next to it, and push the needle through the last bead on that string. Stitch to the decoration to complete the hanging loop.

Metallic festive baubles

*This is a very easy way to make original and striking decorations. Using
a polystyrene ball as the base, you just pin beads and sequins all over it.
If you wish to create a distinct pattern, draw the design on the ball with a
felt-tip pen before you begin inserting the beads.*

You will need

Materials
Ribbon: 10 cm (4 in) x 4 mm (³⁄16 in) wide,
    per bauble
Sewing thread to match ribbon
PVA glue

Small bauble:
Polystyrene ball: 5 cm (2 in) in diameter
Small cup sequins in gold: approx. 300
Small silver pearl beads: approx. 300 x
    3 mm (⅛ in) in diameter
Lill pins: approx. 300 x 13 mm (½ in) long

Large bauble:
Polystyrene ball: 8 cm (3⅛ in) in diameter
Cup sequins in bronze, silver and gold:
    approx. 400
Gold and silver pearl beads: approx. 400 x
    4 mm (³⁄16 in) in diameter
Gold dressmaking pins: approx. 400 x
    2 cm (¾ in) long

Tools
Fine needle
Scissors

How to make

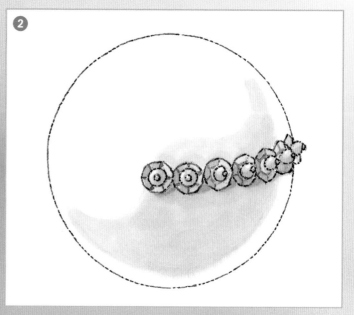

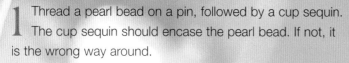

1 Thread a pearl bead on a pin, followed by a cup sequin. The cup sequin should encase the pearl bead. If not, it is the wrong way around.

2 Push the bead and sequin pin into the polystyrene ball. It is best to start at the centre of the ball, at the widest point, and work upwards and downwards from there. Form the first row of sequins and beads, making sure that the edges of the sequins touch or slightly overlap, so that you cannot see the polystyrene ball underneath.

3 Repeat the process to form the next rows of sequins and beads in a contrasting colour. Repeat to cover the whole bauble, but stop before you do the final two rows at the top of the bauble.

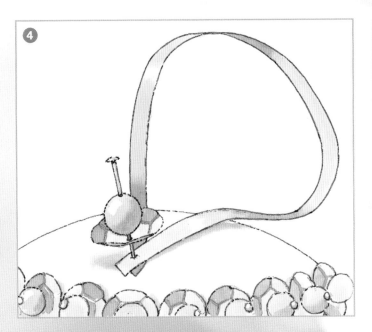

4 To make the hanging loop, fold the length of ribbon in half and secure the ends with a couple of stitches to form a loop. Glue the ends to the top of the bauble and allow to dry. Complete the final two rows of sequins and beads, finishing the bauble and covering the ends of the hanging loop.

Spiral coasters

These spiral coasters will punctuate your table with glowing spots of colour. Long lengths of rocaille beads are laid in a spiral shape and stitched to a backing fabric. Clear glass rocaille beads sparkle when they catch the light, but matt rocaille beads could also be used.

You will need

Materials

Per coaster:

Cardboard

Glass rocaille beads: 2 x 24 g (1 oz) pots

Cotton fabric: 15 x 15 cm (6 x 6 in)

Heavyweight interfacing: 15 x 15 cm (6 x 6 in)

Backing fabric: 15 x 15 cm (6 x 6 in)

Thread

Tools

Drawing compass

Pencil

Fine needle

Scissors

How to make

1 Make the base for the coaster. Draw a circle 12 cm (4¾ in) in diameter on the piece of cardboard and cut it out with the scissors. Make another circle 10 cm (4 in) in diameter. Use the larger circle as a template for the coaster: place it on the square of cotton fabric and draw around it. Cut it out. Place the smaller circle on the wrong side of the circle of fabric, in the centre, and draw around it with a pencil. This inner circle forms the coaster; the border of fabric around it forms a hem.

2 Cut out a circle of interfacing, using the smaller circle as a template. Place the interfacing on the wrong side of the fabric circle. Fold in the hem and oversew in position.

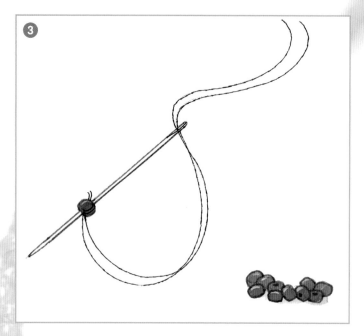

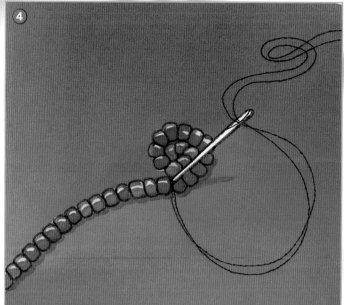

3 Make up a string of rocaille beads 50 cm (19¹¹/₁₆ in) long – this length is easy to work with when sewing the string in a spiral shape. Using a double length of thread, thread on the first rocaille bead. Pass the needle back through the hole of the bead twice more to secure it. Thread on the rest of the beads.

4 Pencil-mark the centre of the coaster. Working from the right side, push the needle through the centre and finish off with a few stitches on the back to secure the beaded strand. Re-thread the needle with a double length of thread and begin to work the beaded strand into a spiral pattern by winding it outwards from the central bead. Make small stitches every four or five beads to hold the strand in place.

5 Continue to wind the strand into a spiral, stitching between the beads to hold them to the fabric. Repeat the process with further strands, until the spiral is 10 cm (4 in) in diameter and covers the coaster.

6 Pull off any beads left on the strand and push the needle to the back of the coaster. Make several stitches to secure the thread, cut off the ends and knot them together.

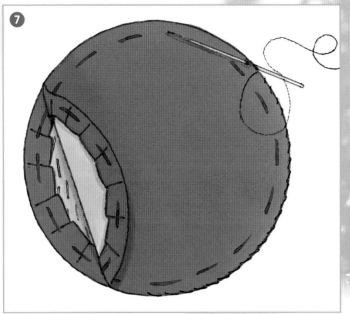

7 Make the backing for the coaster, using cardboard templates as before. Cut a circle of backing fabric 12 cm (4¾ in) in diameter for the backing; mark an inner circle on the back 10 cm (4 in) in diameter, and fold in the 1 cm (⅜ in) hem. Press flat. Place the wrong side of the backing on the wrong side of the coaster and oversew neatly around the edge.

Vintage-style mirror

This chic, bead-embellished mirror is made from an old reclaimed mirror. Old glass, with its slightly distressed look, gives the mirror its vintage style. (If you want to work on a new mirror, visit a glass merchant and buy a piece of mirror with polished edges.) Glass beads create a floral border.

You will need

Materials
Mirror: approx. 80 x 62 cm (31½ x 24½ in)
Octagonal faceted beads: 50
Large pearl beads: 10
Large glass flowers: 15
Small glass flowers: 10
Small round glass beads: 25
Glass leaves: 24
Strong glue suitable for sticking glass

How to make

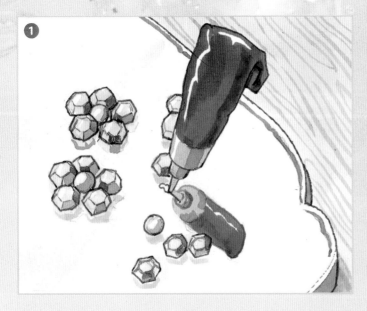

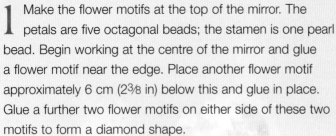

1 Make the flower motifs at the top of the mirror. The petals are five octagonal beads; the stamen is one pearl bead. Begin working at the centre of the mirror and glue a flower motif near the edge. Place another flower motif approximately 6 cm (2⅜ in) below this and glue in place. Glue a further two flower motifs on either side of these two motifs to form a diamond shape.

2 Add four more flower motifs along the top edge of the mirror, spaced apart equally. Glue one flower motif in each of the bottom corners of the mirror.

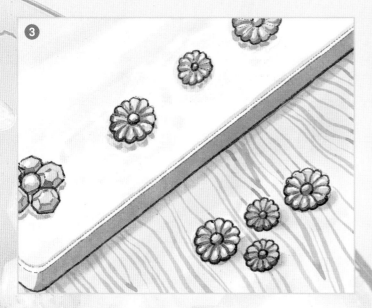

3 Glue the flower-shaped beads down the sides and along the bottom of the mirror, about 6 cm (2⅜ in) apart, alternating large and small beads. Glue four large glass flowers between the flower motifs along the top. Glue a small round glass bead in the centre of each flower-shaped bead.

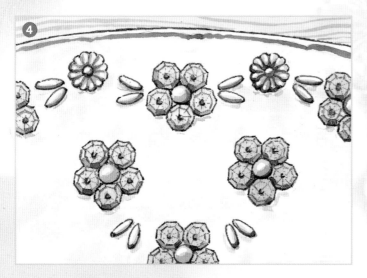

4 Glue on pairs of leaf shapes, at a slight angle to each other, as shown above.

Ethnic photo album

Sumptuous green raw silk is trimmed with a sari-style ribbon and oversewn with glass rocaille beads and bugle beads, to create this stunning fabric cover for a photo album. Glittering rocaille paisley motifs echo the pattern on the ribbon, while the pretty blue tassel features chunky glass beads.

You will need

Materials

Green raw silk to fit the dimensions of the
    album, plus 10 cm (4 in) around all edges
Decorative ribbon to fit back and front of
    album, plus 10 cm (4 in) either side
Green glass rocaille beads: 240
Turquoise glass rocaille beads: 280
Pale turquoise glass rocaille beads: 80
Light blue short bugle beads: 160
Large glass beads: 2
Blue embroidery thread in three shades:
    3 skeins x 8 m (8¾ yd)
Ribbon to attach tassel: 15 cm x 3 mm
    (6 x ⅛ in)
Matching and contrasting sewing thread
Fabric glue
Paper (optional): 2 pieces, dimensions as
    album covers but 1 cm (⅜ in) smaller
    on the three outer edges.
Cardboard

Tools

Fine needle
Soft pencil (preferably white)
Scissors

How to make

1 Tack the decorative ribbon across the middle of the silk fabric (it will run across the centre of the album) and hand-stitch in place. Sew a row of green rocaille beads along the top and bottom edges of the ribbon, spacing the beads approximately 5 mm (3/16 in) apart. Sew a further row of green rocaille beads 2 mm (1/16 in) below each row, with the beads approximately 5 mm (3/16 in) apart, staggering them with the row next to them. Sew a row of light blue short bugle beads inside the rows of green rocaille beads, spacing the beads approximately 6 mm (1/4 in) apart, then sew a row of pale turquoise rocaille beads along the middle of the decorative ribbon, spacing the beads approximately 6 mm (1/4 in) apart.

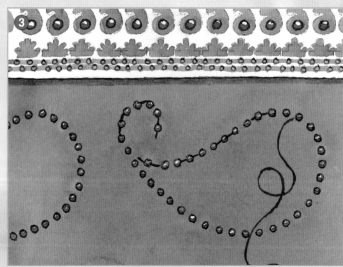

2 Draw a paisley template on the piece of cardboard and cut it out. Place the template at regular intervals in a line on the wrong side of the fabric, both above and below the decorative ribbon and, with the soft pencil, mark out the paisley motifs. Tack around these motifs with contrasting sewing thread so that they are clearly visible on the right side of the fabric.

3 On the right side of the fabric, sew on turquoise glass rocaille beads to follow the shape of the paisley motifs, spacing the beads 5 mm (3/16 in) apart. Unpick the contrasting sewing thread.

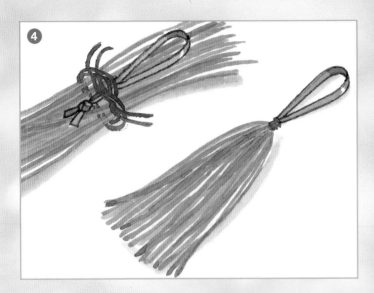

4 To make the tassel, cut the blue thread into 20 cm (8 in) lengths and lay flat. Knot the ends of the thin ribbon to form a loop. Place the knot on the blue threads. Tie two lengths of thread around the bunch of threads just above the knot in the ribbon. Wind the thread around tightly to hold the tassel securely. Fold the top lengths of blue thread back over the lower ones to form the tassel.

5 Thread two large glass beads one after the other on to the ribbon loop, just above the knot.

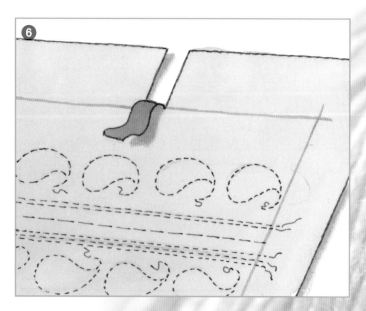

6 Now cover the album. Place the fabric flat on the table with the wrong side uppermost and lay the open album on top. Snip the fabric above the spine of the album, from the raw edge down to the spine, to create a flap. Do this at the top and bottom of the spine.

7 Remove the album. Fold each flap of fabric down and press flat. Glue in place. Attach the tassel. Place the loop on the spine and glue in place.

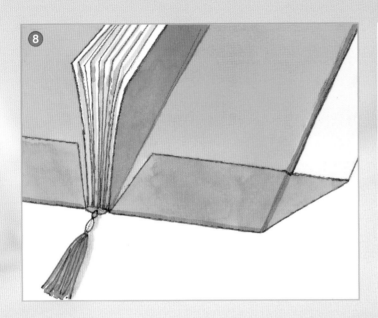

8 Place the album back on the fabric, holding the leaves and the back cover at an angle of 90°. Allow the front cover to rest on the fabric. Fold the edges of the fabric over the front cover and glue in place, folding in the corners neatly as you do so. Follow the same method for the back cover.

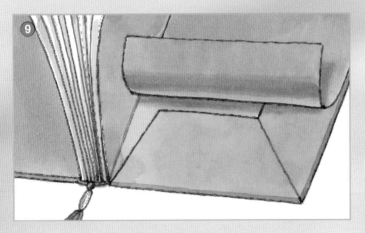

9 For a neater finish, glue a sheet of paper to the inside of the front and back covers to conceal the raw edges of the fabric. The paper should be approximately 1 cm (3/8 in) smaller, on the three outer edges, than the album.

Baroque treasure box

A glamorous box in rich shades of red, mauve and green adds baroque splendour to a dressing table. Its jewelled appearance makes it the perfect receptacle for treasured items. Use faceted glass and plastic beads, applied in a floral design. Velvet ribbons add further opulence.

You will need

Materials

Box: 15 x 15 x 8 cm (6 x 6 x 3⅛ in)

Acrylic paint: mauve

Small round faceted beads: 12 red;
  6 purple; 12 amber

Lozenge-shaped flat beads: 20 red; 8 green

Octagonal flat beads: 4 mauve

Medium-sized round faceted beads:
  20 olive green

Medium-sized oval faceted beads: 10 purple;
  10 yellow green; 10 blue green; 11 red

Strong glue suitable for glass and plastic

Dark red velvet ribbon: 65 cm (25⅝ in),
  1.5 cm (⁹⁄₁₆ in) wide

Plum velvet ribbon: 65 cm (25⅝ in), 1.5 cm
  (⁹⁄₁₆ in) wide

Purple velvet ribbon: 65 cm (25⅝ in), 2 cm
  (¾ in) wide

Fabric glue

Tools

Scissors

Paintbrush

Pencil

How to make

1 Paint the box with the mauve acrylic paint and allow it to dry thoroughly.

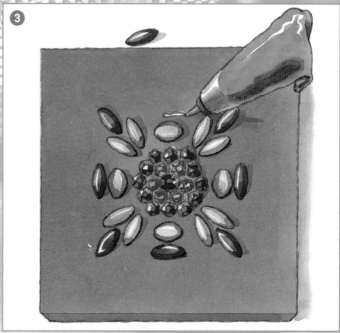

2 Make the central flower motif. Pencil-mark the centre of the lid, to indicate where the centre of the flower will be. Glue on the beads. Use one red medium-sized oval faceted bead for the centre of the flower. Surround it with small round faceted beads: an inner ring of six purple beads and an outer ring of twelve red beads.

3 Now make the pattern around the central flower motif. Arrange the four mauve octagonal flat beads around the central flower and glue in place. Apply 'leaves' between these: use the green lozenge-shaped flat beads and glue two between each of the mauve beads, pointing outwards at a slight angle to each other. Glue a red lozenge-shaped flat bead between the angle of each leaf, then add four more, sticking them to lie parallel to the mauve beads.

4 Each edge of the lid features four flowers. Pencil-mark the flower centres, spaced an equal distance apart. Glue on the central beads for each flower: use the amber small round faceted beads. Surround the central bead with five beads to make the flower petals. Use the olive green, medium-sized round faceted beads, and the yellow green, blue green, purple and red medium-sized oval faceted beads.

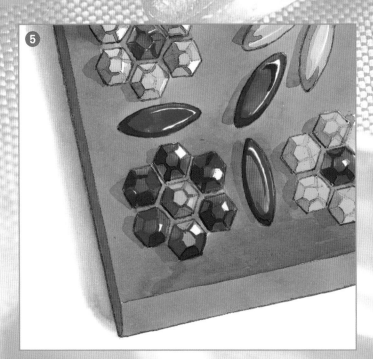

5 Glue a red lozenge-shaped flat bead between each of the flowers around the edge. Allow all the glued beads to dry thoroughly.

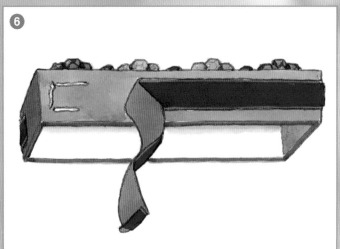

6 Trim the box. Stick the dark red ribbon around the edge of the lid with fabric glue, turning in the raw edges to prevent fraying.

7 With the lid on the box, glue the lengths of plum and purple ribbon around the sides of the box, approximately 5 mm (3/16 in) apart, turning in the edges as before.

Other ideas
Cover the box with fabric, instead of painting it, before you apply the beads. Try using a selection of wooden beads for a different effect.

Index

A B

acrylic paint 136, 138
baubles, metallic festive 118–21
bead hangers 11
bead shops, specialist 8
beaded fringes 11, 36–41,
  42–5, 46–8, 50
beading basics 10–11
beading needles 11
bird motifs 115
bolster, glamorous 26–31
bookmarks 72
boxes
  Baroque treasure box 136–41
  bead storage 8
  decorative 72
  jewellery 8
bracelets 8
bugle beads 8, 16

C

candles, and safety 79, 84, 108
candlesticks 86
chandeliers
  beaded chandelier 58–63
  decorations 86
Christmas stockings 115
Christmas trees 115
circular shapes 32, 34, 124, 125
cleaning beads 8
coasters
  Moroccan-style 102–5
  spiral 122–5
coffee spoons, flower 72–5
cotton 10

craft shops 8
curtain, beaded taffeta 36–41
cushion cover, home-made 24,
  25
cushions 10
  glamorous bolster 26–31
  modern linen cushion 32–5
  tropical cushion cover 22–5

D E

decorations
  metallic festive baubles 118–21
  Shaker-style festive decorations
    114–17
dressmaking pins 11
dressmaking scissors 10
embroidery 8, 10
epoxy glue 11
eye pins 11

F

fabric glue 11
faceted beads 17
felt 115, 116
flea markets, as small bead sources
  8
flowers
  beaded flower shapes 46, 49
  decorating 24, 25
  flower motifs 128, 129, 138, 139
  flower-shaped beads 77, 80, 127,
    129
  wirework 56, 57, 72–5
fringes, beaded 11, 36–41, 42–5,
  46–8, 50

G H I

glass beads 8, 12, 19
glue 10, 11
greetings cards 72
haberdashery departments 8
hanging loops 117, 121
headwires 11
heart shapes 115–17
instant bond glue 11

L

lampshade, French-style 98–101
leaves
  decorating 24
  wirework 56, 57
lighting 10
lill pins 11
linen 32, 42, 46, 49

M N

materials 10–11
mirror, vintage-style 126–9
napkin rings
  chunky spiral 68–71
  fancy bead 92–5
necklaces 8, 92
needle-nosed pliers 10, 11
needles 8, 10, 11
nightlight holders, beaded 106–9
nylon thread 10, 11

O P

online suppliers 8
paint, acrylic 136, 138
paisley motifs 130, 132

pearl beads 8, 13

photo album, ethnic 130–35

picture frame, fun 110–113

pins 11

plastic beads 12, 13

pleats 40

pliers 8, 11

  needle-nosed 10

polystyrene balls 11, 118, 120

pretty accents 96–141

  Baroque treasure box 136–41

  beaded nightlight holders
    106–9

  ethnic photo album 130–35

  French-style lampshade 98–101

  fun picture frame 110–113

  metallic festive baubles 118–21

  Moroccan-style coasters 102–5

  Shaker-style festive decorations
    114–17

  spiral coasters 122–5

  vintage-style mirror 126–9

PVA glue 11

R

ribbons

  bow 98, 100

  embroidered 107, 108,
    109

  hanging loops 121

  motifs 27, 28

  sari-style 130, 132, 133

  trim 46, 49

  velvet 136, 140

rocaille beads 8, 11, 14–15

S

salad servers, wrapped 64–7

sales, as small bead sources 8

scissors 8, 10

secondhand shops, as small
  bead sources 8

seed beads 8

sequins 8, 10, 16

sewing machine 10

sewing thread 10, 11

silk 10, 130

soft furnishings 20–51

  beaded taffeta curtain 36–41

  elegant throw 46–51

  glamorous bolster 26–31

  modern linen cushion 32–5

  summer table runner 42–5

  tropical cushion cover 22–5

star shapes 114–17

superglue 11

T V

table runner, summer
  42–5

taffeta 37

tape measure 10

tassels 27, 28, 30, 31, 130,
  133, 134

throws 10

  elegant throw 46–51

tiebacks, flower 54–7

tools 10–11

vase decorations 86–91

velvet 10, 27, 28, 136

votives, spiral beaded 82–5

W

wall sconce 76–81

wire 8, 10, 11

  coloured 64

  copper 11

  gauges 11

  gold 11

  silver 11

wire cutters 10

wirework 52–95

  beaded chandelier 58–63

  chunky spiral napkin rings
    68–71

  fancy bead napkin rings 92–5

  flower coffee spoons 72–5

  flower tiebacks 54–7

  spiral beaded votives 82–5

  vase decorations 86–91

  wall sconce 76–81

  wrapped salad servers 64–7

wooden beads 18

Acknowledgements

Picture acknowledgements

Special photography © Octopus Publishing Group Limited
/Sandra Lane.

Other photography © Octopus Publishing Group Limited
/Graham Atkins-Hughes 10, 11, 13, 14-15 top, 16 top left,
17, 18 top left, 19 top left.

Executive Editor Katy Denny
Editor Leanne Bryan
Executive Art Editor Karen Sawyer
Designer Janis Utton
Illustrator Kate Simunek
Photographer Sandra Lane
Stylist Catherine Woram
Picture Library Assistant Taura Riley
Production Controller Nigel Reed